I0709583

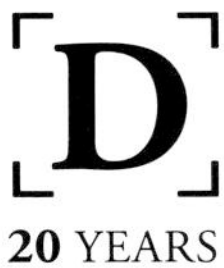

20 YEARS

Cofounders: Taj Forer and Michael Itkoff
Creative Director: Ursula Damm
Copy Editor: Gabrielle Fastman

ISBN: 978-1-954119-29-1

Printed by Ofset Yapimevi, Turkey

Daylight Books
E-mail: info@daylightbooks.org
Web: www.daylightbooks.org

The Quetzal
A feathered serpent
Moving between worlds
Mirroring a language
That weaves between planes
Slowly spreading across decades
Taking new forms depending
On who can wield it best
Serpent Tongue

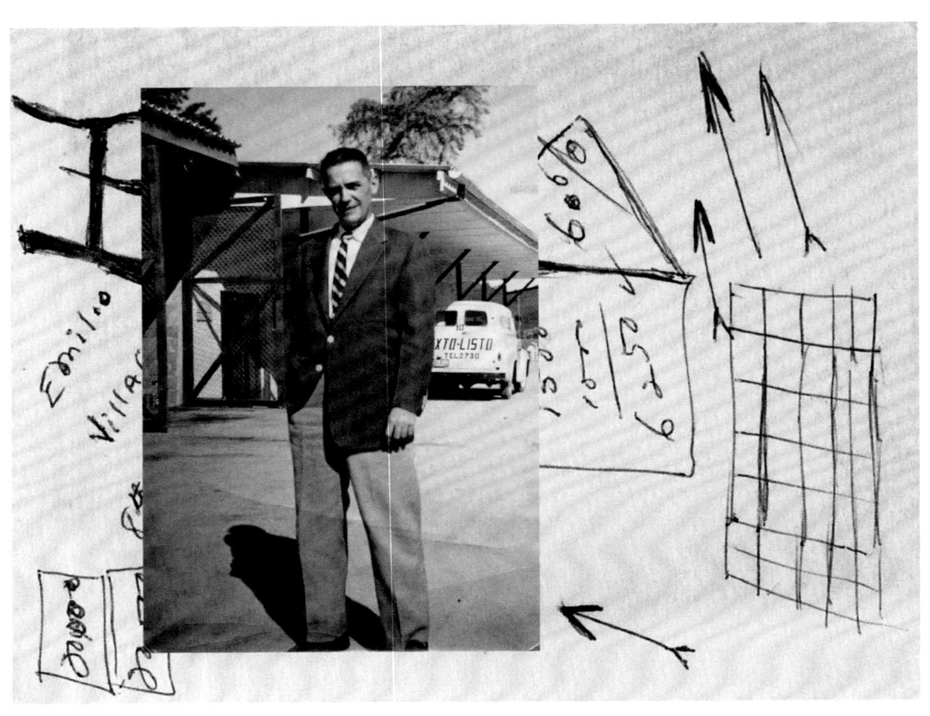

SECRET
SECURITY INFORMATION

25 September 1953

MEMORANDUM

2003

SUBJECT: TASKS FOR CHIEF OF STATION, GUATEMALA

1. Your priorities for development of KUFIRE assets are as follows:

a. Controlled penetration of the Communist Party.

b. Controlled penetrations of the major labor unions.

c. Controlled penetrations in the major anti-Communist organizations.

d. Controlled penetrations in the armed forces, or controlled agents with access to current planning both in senior and junior officer groups.

e. Controlled agents with access to high-level Guatemalan Government political propaganda planning.

2. The Station will transmit any rumors re: ARBENZ government officials, actions taken or to be taken by the Army, government - army relationships, revolutionary activities, relationships among the Communists and any bad morale factors among the ruling clique to Headquarters. The rumors will be accompanied by Station comments re plausibility, where rumor was overheard and any suggested restrictions on re-use in other countries throughout the Hemisphere. (Weekly report, unless no rumors are overheard.)

3. The Station will clip and send, with appropriate comments, the column, "Boqueras" to Headquarters whenever it contains rumors of value to the anti-Guatemalan campaign.

4. ESCONSON I will write a "psychological barometer" report on local conditions, PW activities, ~~and give ideas on possible PW actions.~~ This report will be sent Headquarters each week.

5. The Station will make a continuing study of morale factors (complaints, desires, etc.) among the following groups:

a. Students
b. Laborers (farm & industrial)
c. Army Officers
d. Enlisted Men
e. Government Officials
f. Farmers — owners & operators
g. Business and professional men

As complete a report as possible on each group should be in Headquarters o/a 15 November 1953. Thereafter Morale Factors should be included with the Rumor Report.

SECRET

INTRODUCTION

Annie Grossinger has used forensic anthropology tools to try to reconstruct the life and career of John Dougherty, her maternal grandfather, who was linked to the 1954 CIA-sponsored coup in Guatemala. By combining CIA and other archival documents along with her own familial and professional photographs, Grossinger has tried to uncover the degree of her grandfather's involvement in the coup. According to conservative Guatemalan Fernando Sandoval, whose parents were friends with Dougherty, "John was special because he had a hard line. He didn't want to compromise with the Communists."

The CIA claimed President Jacobo Árbenz Guzmán was a Communist because he expropriated fallow United Fruit Company land (actually the Árbenz government paid $1.2 million based on the land's existing tax value); bought arms from Czechoslovakia (the US refused to sell him weapons); and permitted several avowed Communists in his cabinet. To most Guatemalans, even to right-leaning Peruvian Nobelist Mario Vargas Llosa, Árbenz may have been Guatemala's Abraham Lincoln. But because of the coup, Guatemala endured thirty-six years of armed conflict and the death of nearly 200,000 citizens, many of them innocent Indigenous people.

Serpent Tongue is a personal journey to understand Dougherty's life from the brittle, broken pieces of a kaleidoscopic puzzle. Grossinger's photographs and interviews of progressive and conservative Guatemalans bring her grandfather into focus, but the image is fuzzy and elusive; disillusioned. Her landscape, portrait, and still-life photographs clash with and complement the archival and personal photographs of seventy years ago. Her lens reveals the hauntingly beautiful texture of battered Guatemalan lives. Like a colorful Cubist painting, this book is a collage of images that teases out the truth of who her grandfather was—something we may never know, despite the trek through a vale of tears.

Serpent Tongue reminds us that the US government has employed "fake news" to achieve its larger political and economic goals for decades in Guatemala, Iran, the Dominican Republic, and elsewhere. Grossinger's book is essential reading for those of us who want to make sure that past mistakes, leading to catastrophic results, are not repeated.

—David Unger

Writer and translator David Unger is the recipient of Guatemala's 2014 Miguel Angel Asturias National Literature Prize for lifetime achievement.

Actual Invasion, Late June 1954

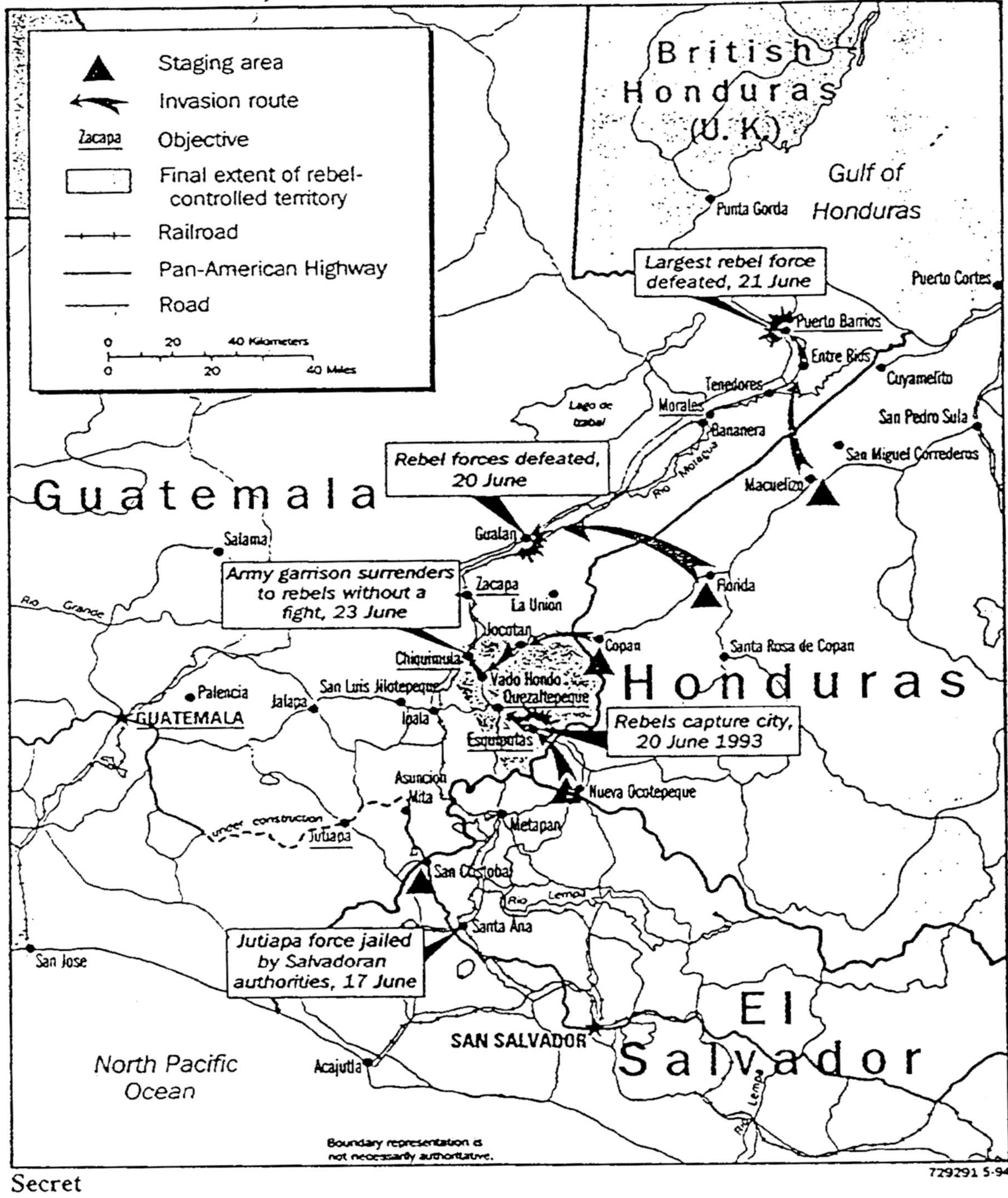

Secret"

In 1954, during the height of the Cold War, the CIA carried out a coup to overthrow the first democratically elected president in Guatemala. It was a turning point for the organization, laying the foundation for a new kind of imperialism in Latin America. In the months leading up to the coup, the CIA station chief in Guatemala City was my grandfather, John Dougherty—a man who died long before I was born but whose presence loomed like a mythological creature throughout much of my childhood.

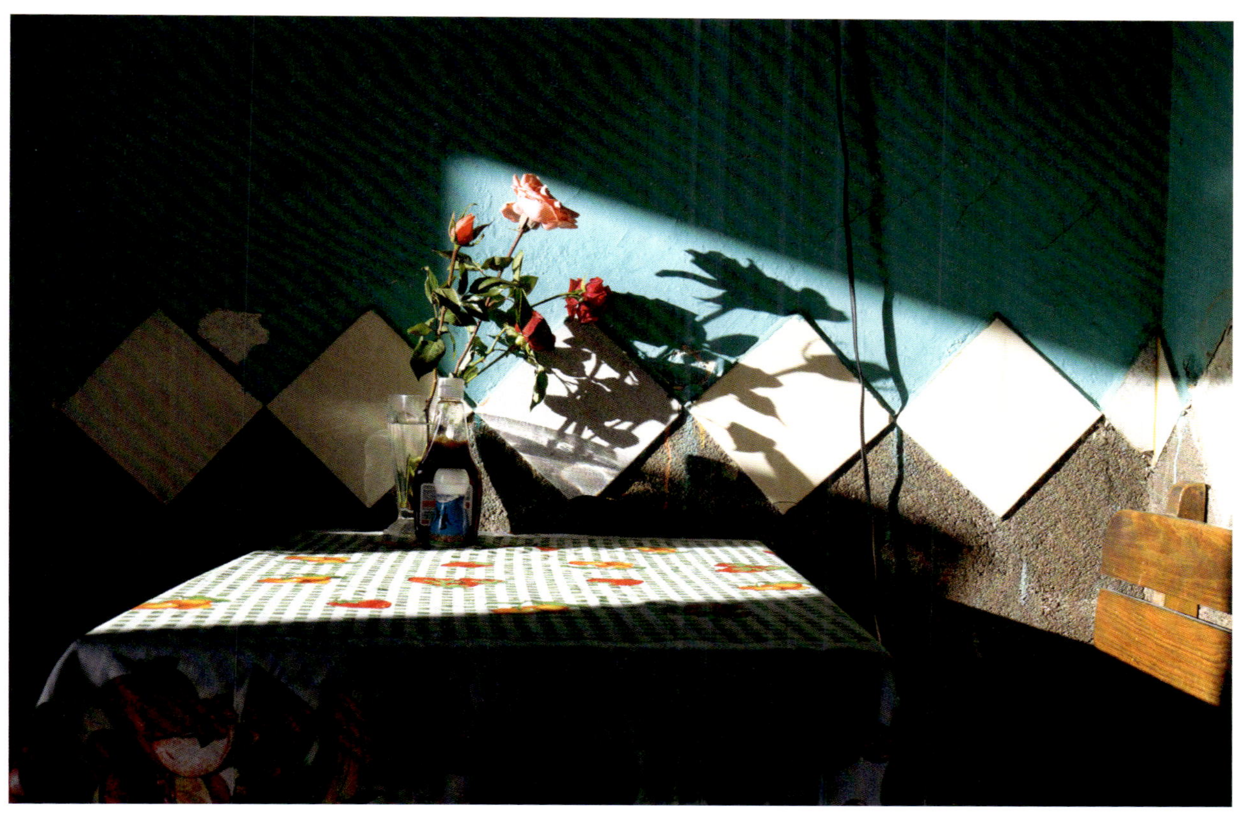

"The roses are blooming," the elites were alerted over Tropical Radio. Leave Guatemala City; the coup was underway.

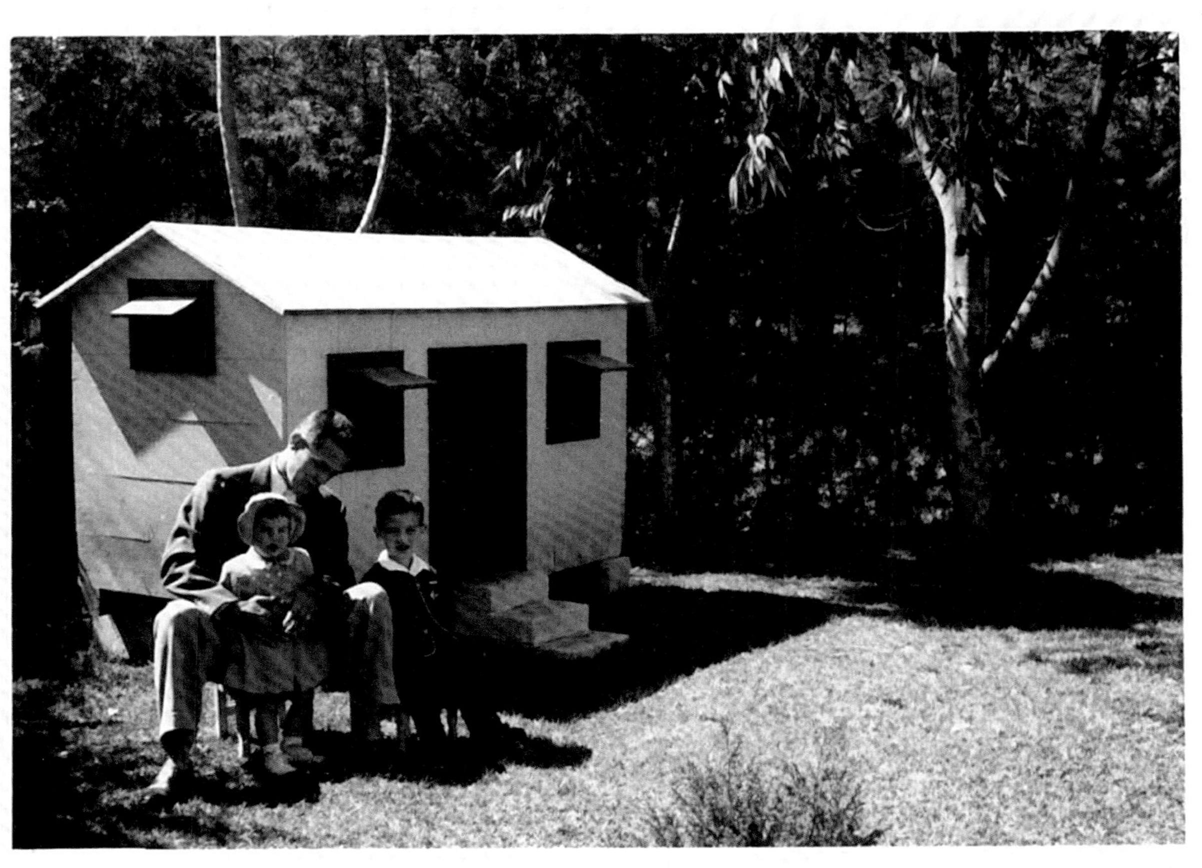

My grandfather with my mother, Maren, and her brother in Guatemala.

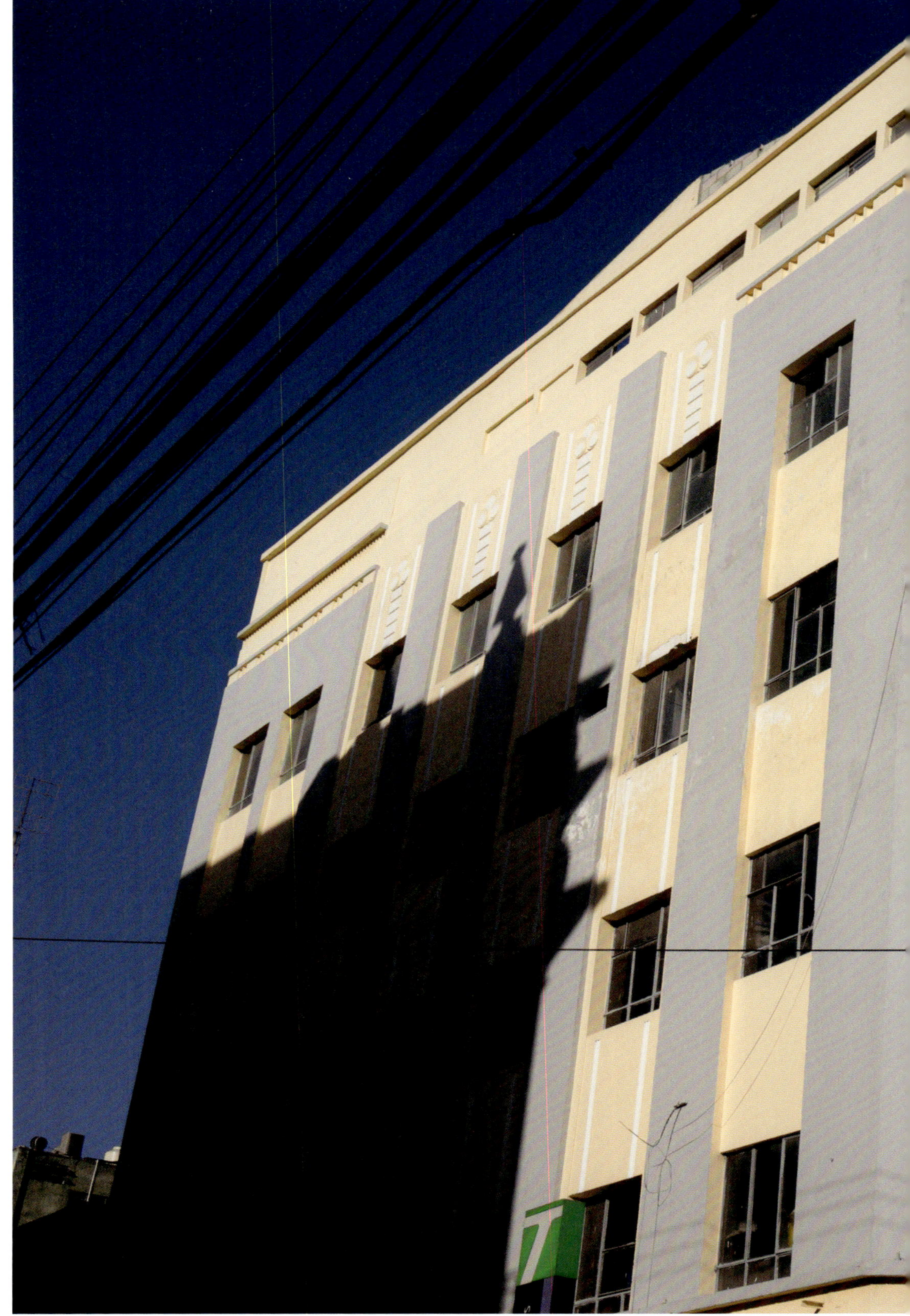

The CIA used a high-powered radio station on the fourth floor of the US embassy building to disseminate its propaganda. Zona 1, Guatemala City, 2019.

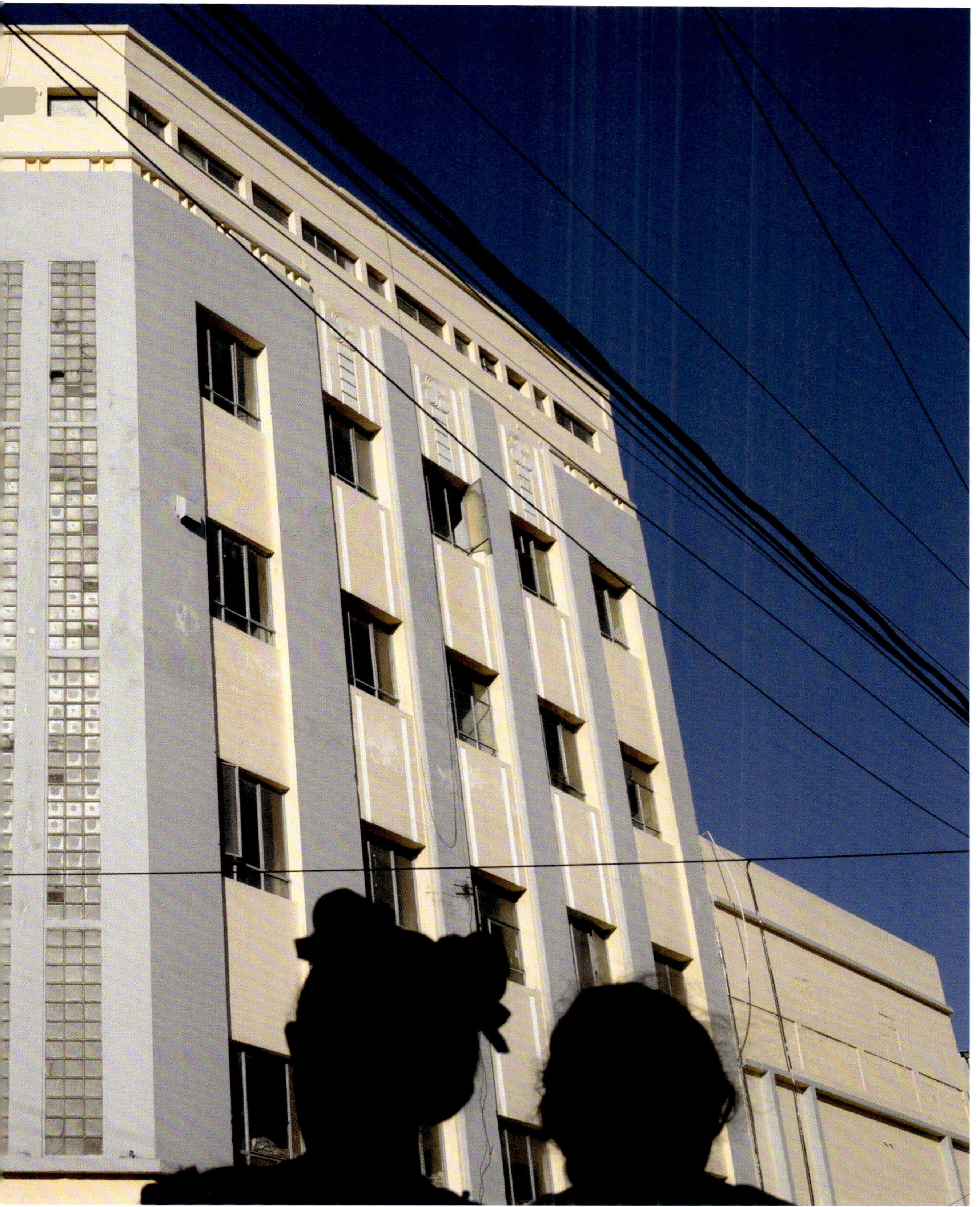

SECRET
SECURITY INFORMATION

ER 2 513

ER 2-3513

14 November 1951

MEMORANDUM TO: Mr. James Lay, Executive Secretary
National Security Council

SUBJECT : [   ]

[   ]
visited CIA on 2 November. In a conversation with Mr. Dulles and
other interested officials in the Agency, [   ] acting as a
spokesman for the United Fruit Company and the Electric Bond and
Share Company, offered the facilities and personnel of these two
organizations to assist CIA in any current or proposed operations
which we may conduct to combat the growth of Communism in Guatemala.

CIA is very interested in this offer and will pursue the matter
further through direct contact with the officials of the United
Fruit Company with whom we are already working in another connection.

Thanks very much for your help in setting up this meeting with
[   ]

SIGNED

[   ]
Assistant to the Director

HJMuller:aml
Orig & 1 - addressee
1 cc   - reading
1 cc   - official
1 cc   [   ] - Western Hemisphere

SECRET

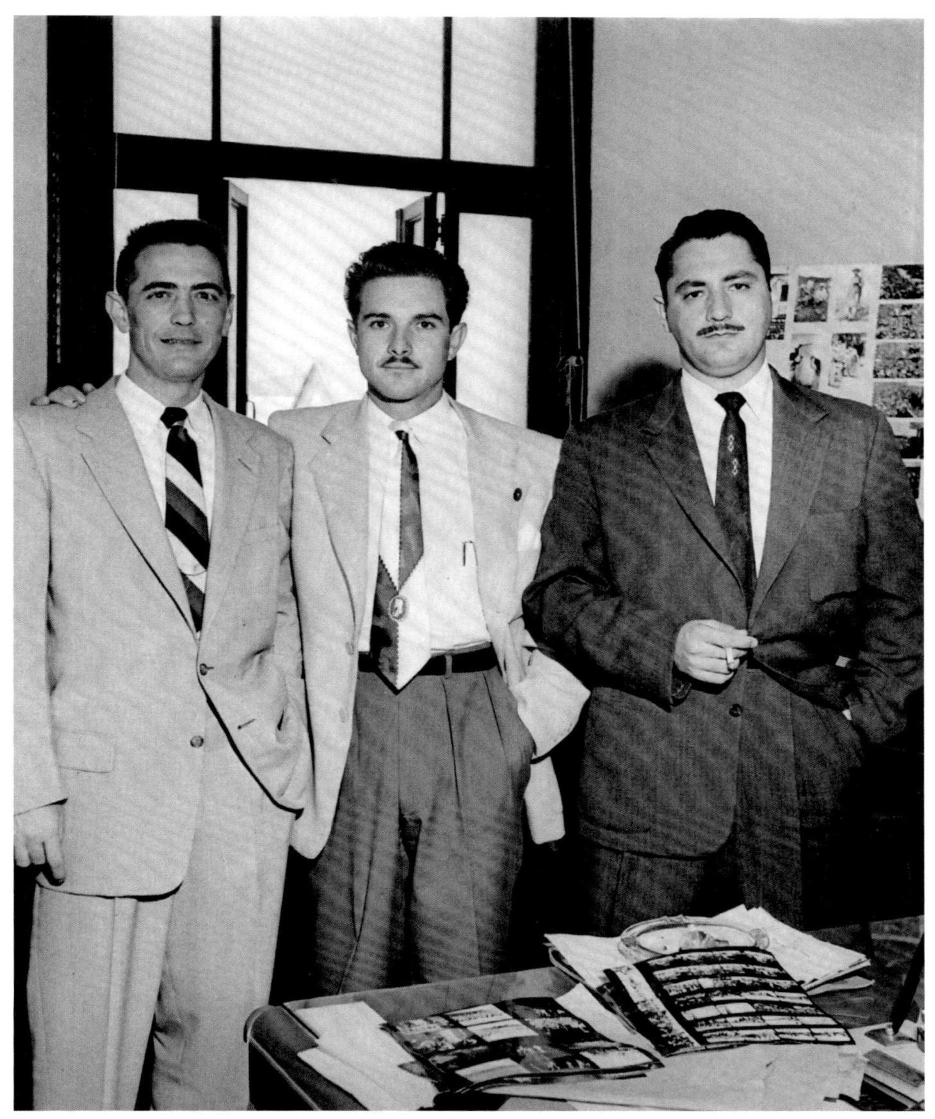

Left to right: My grandfather, John Dougherty, and possible CIA officers Kiki Salazar and Joe Sancho. (Names as annotated by my grandmother decades later.)

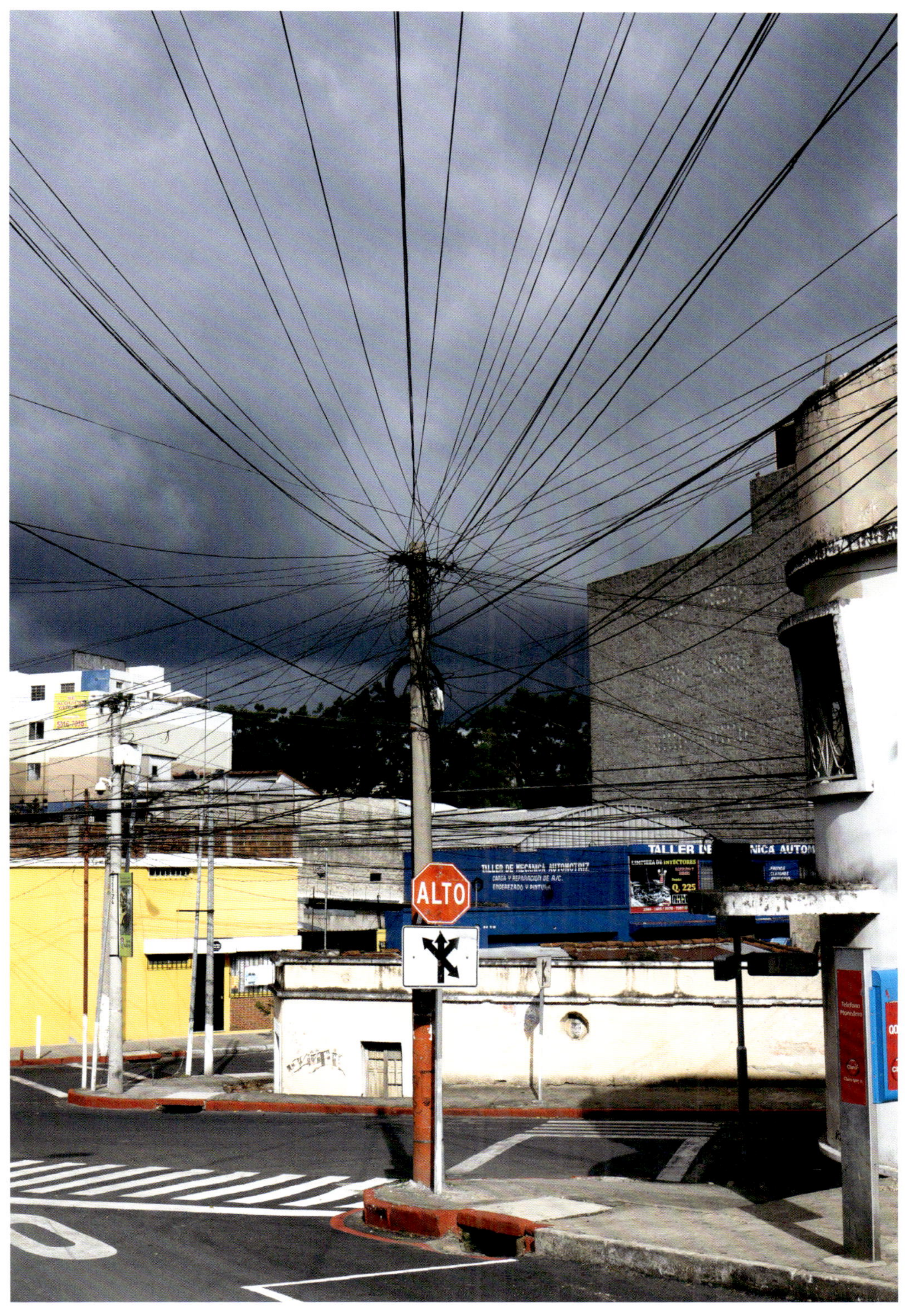

ALTO
TALLER DE MECANICA AUTOMOTRIZ
TALLER LE   NICA AUTOM
Q. 225

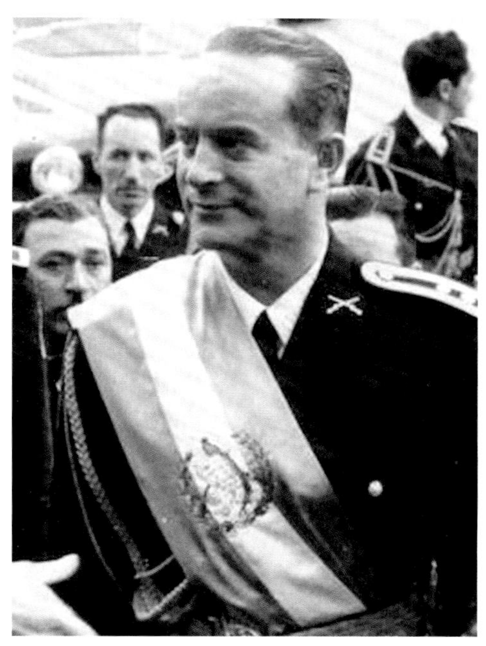

President Jacobo Árbenz Guzmán

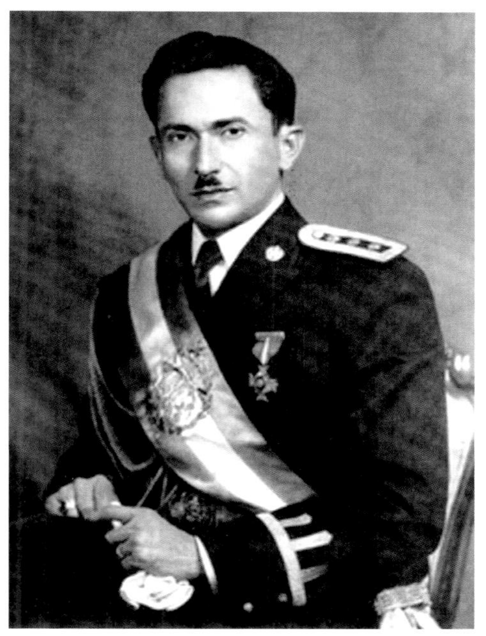

President Carlos Castillo Armas

The Guatemalan Revolution was bookmarked by coups. In 1944, President Jacobo Árbenz Guzmán helped oust the dictator Jorge Ubico Castañeda to install democratic elections, and a decade later, President Carlos Castillo Armas would help the United States overthrow him. The period between, called the Ten Years of Spring, saw the most progressive social, political, and agrarian reforms. But the fear of Communism was heightened. It was during this period that the CIA began to experiment with disinformation and scare tactics, ultimately aimed at wielding power in the region and winning the Cold War.

"It's an ongoing cycle that generates contradictions: a modern economy but an imprisoned society. 1944–1954 was a time of experimentation, but the elites didn't like it.…It's the karma of Guatemala. Change will be small, especially now, and change is dependent on the US."

—Carlos Roberto Sarti

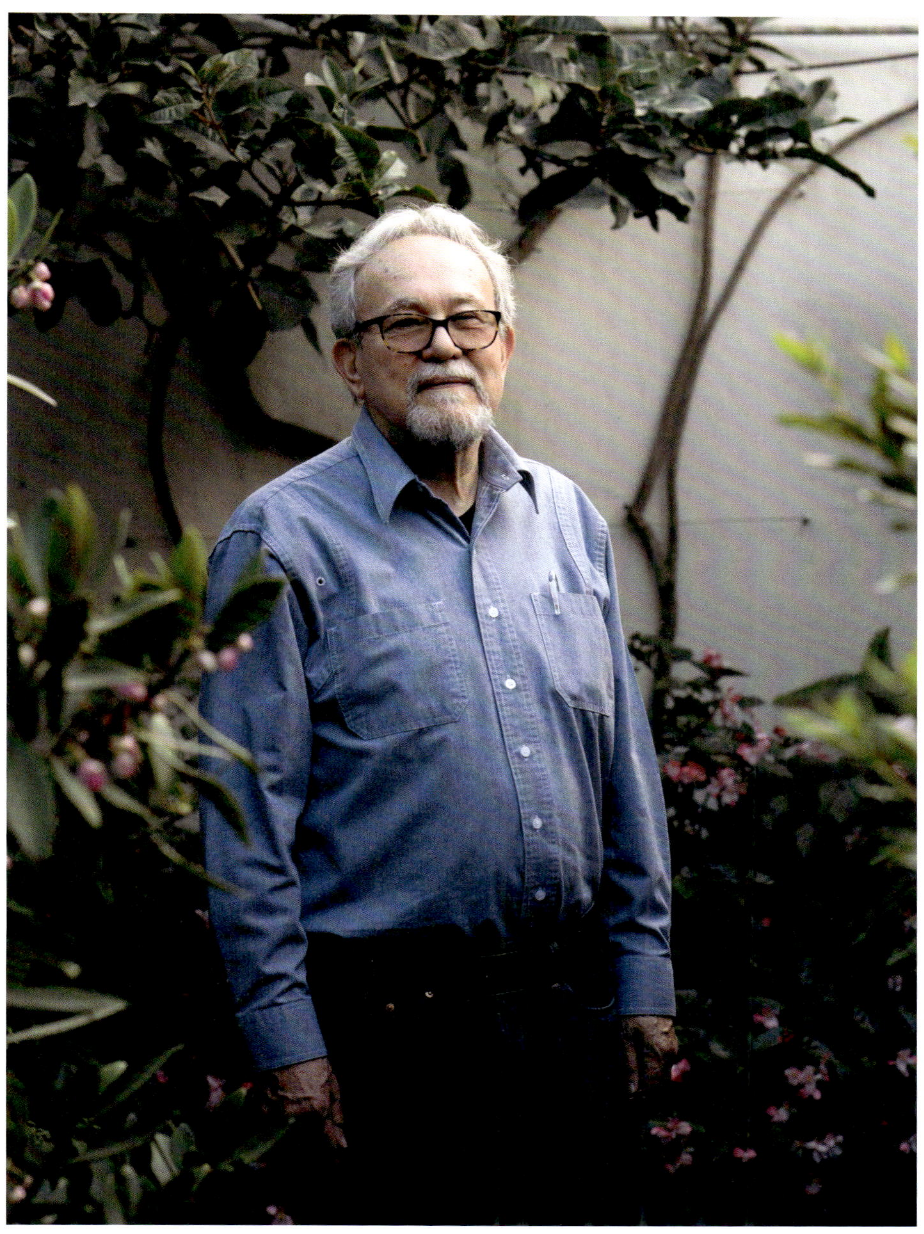

Carlos Roberto Sarti's father and uncle were killed after organizing a resistance against Castillo Armas in 1957. The army placed their bodies outside of a military base so that it looked like they had been attacking the base, in order to justify their murders. After, Carlos took part in the citizen's uprising against an autocratic administration in 1962 and was forced into exile from 1970–1977.

"John Dougherty was a great man. He was trying to liberate Guatemala from Communism because he understood Communism was a type of cancer. That once it stuck in one place, it would start to spread."

—Fernando Sandoval

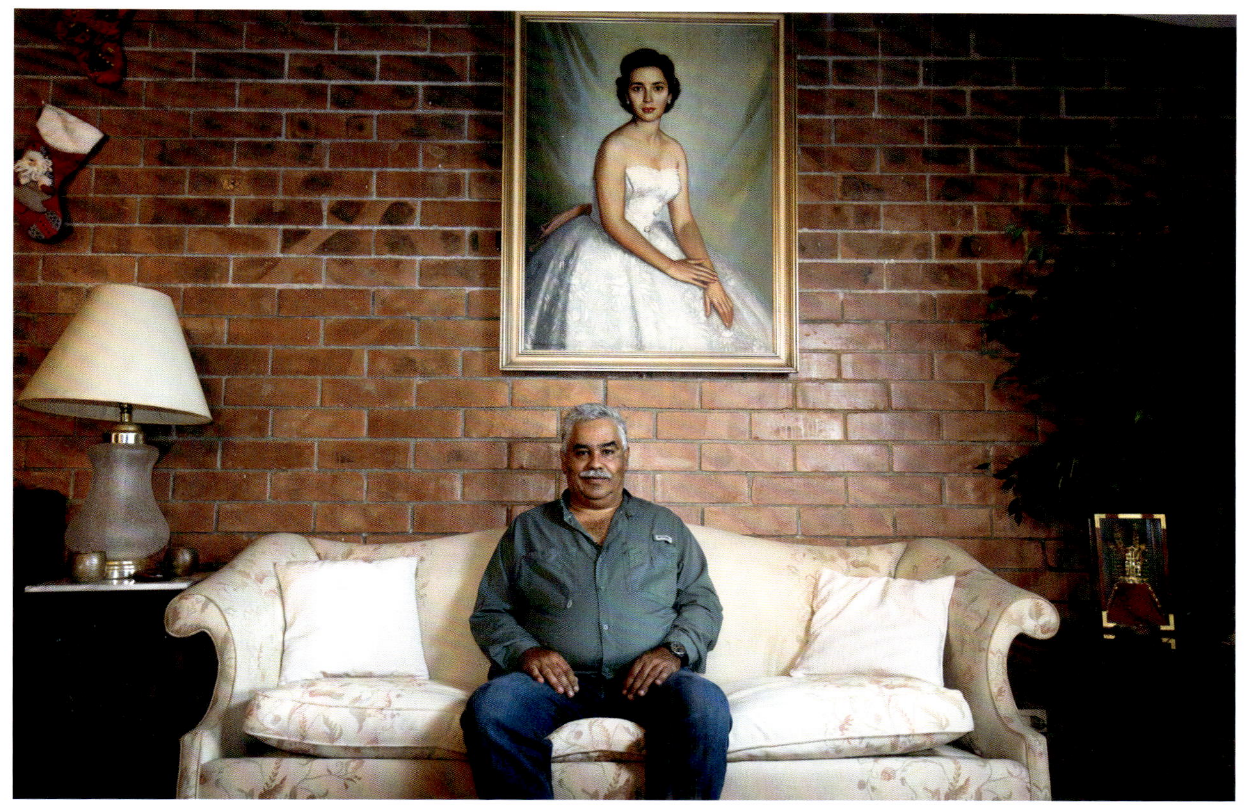

Fernando Sandoval is the son of María and Mario Sandoval Alarcón, who were friends with my grandparents. During the coup, Mario was a student leader in favor of Castillo Armas. It was alleged that his student group received funding from the CIA to aid in their resistance. Once Castillo Armas was in power, he became the leader of the right-wing military group Movimiento de Liberación Nacional (MLN). The MLN would later operate the death squads that killed an estimated 200,000 people, mostly Indigenous, in acts of genocide during the Guatemalan Civil War .

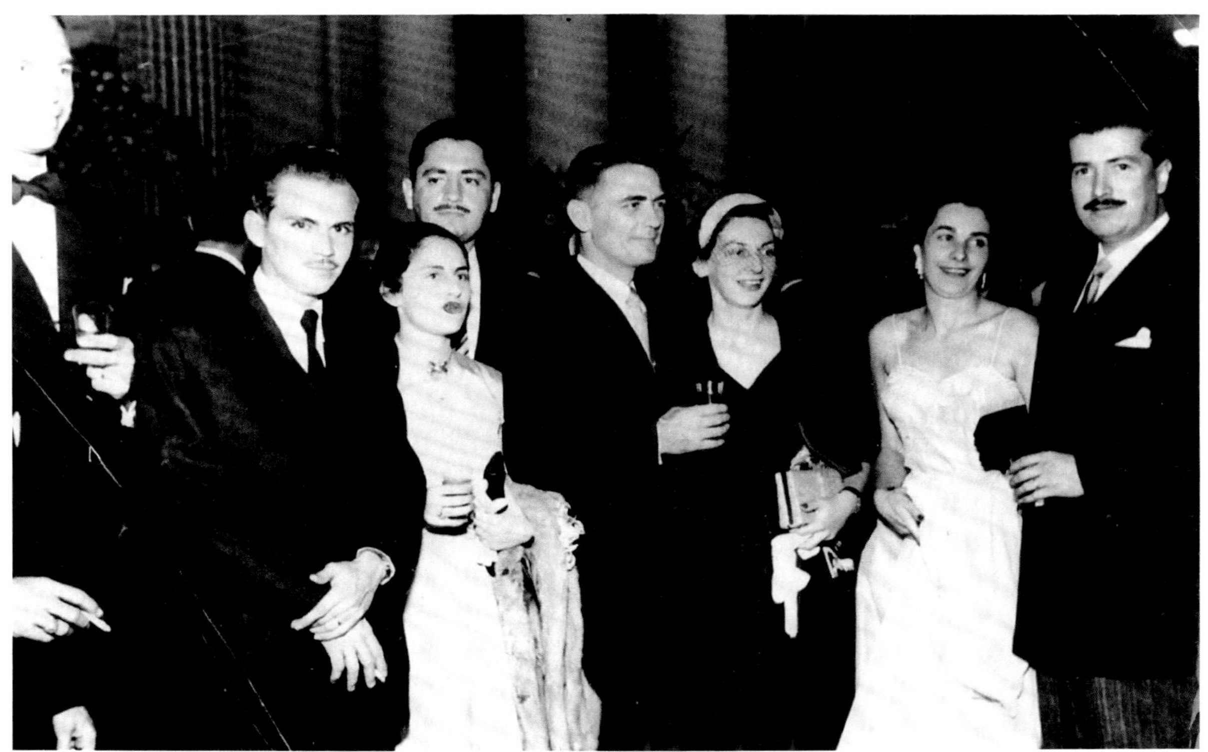

John and my grandmother, Josephine (center), at an event with other officers and members of Guatemalan society.

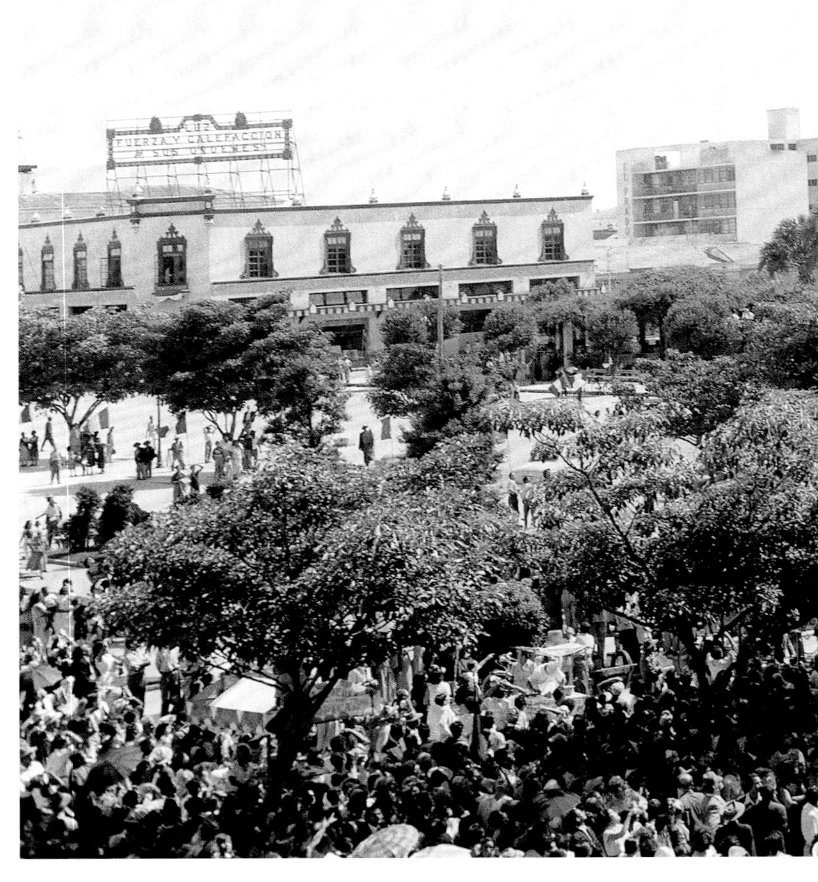

In the weeks leading up to the coup, the CIA flew low-flying planes over Guatemala City in order to instill fear and ignite chaos. But instead of bombs, they dropped anti-Communist propaganda.

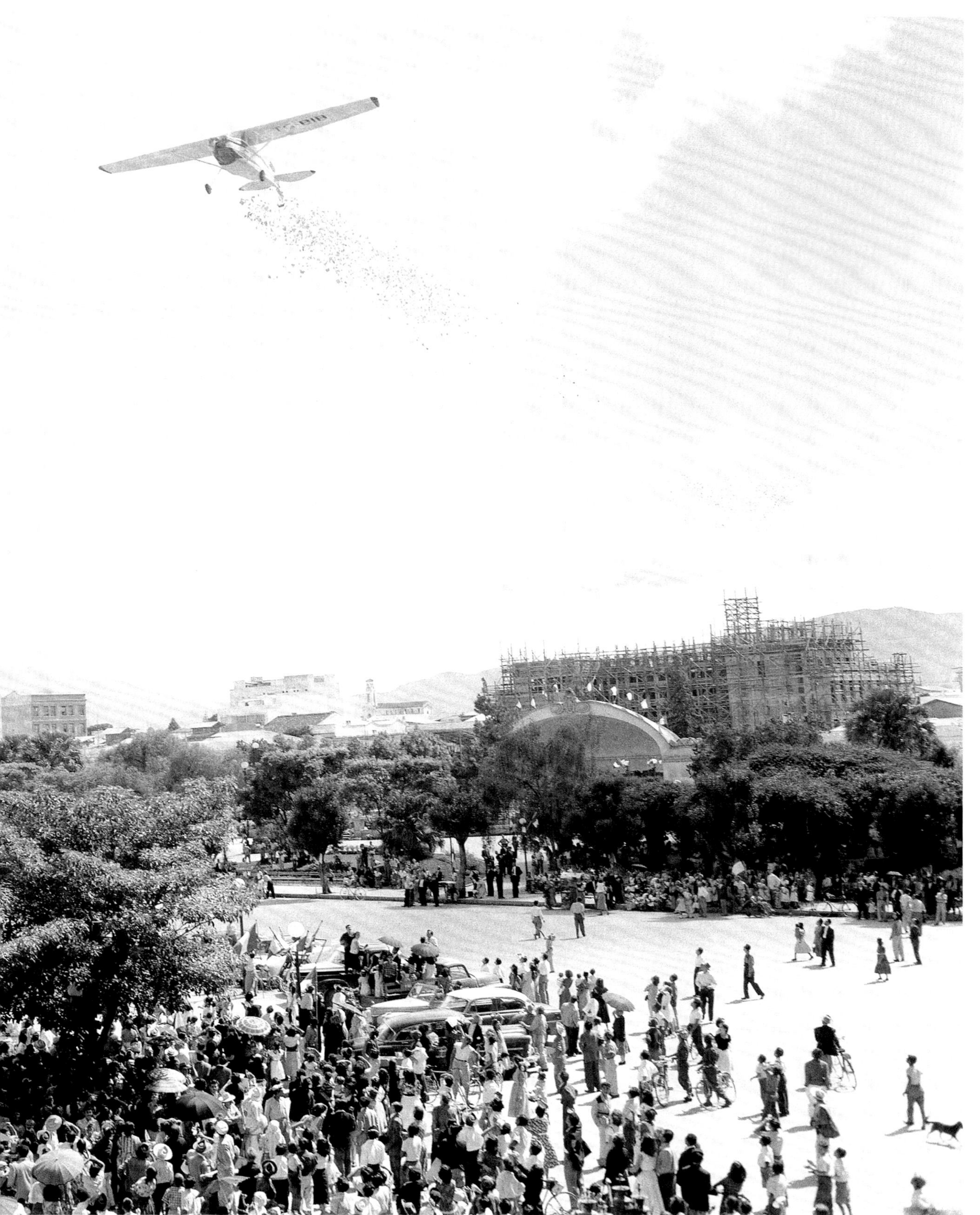

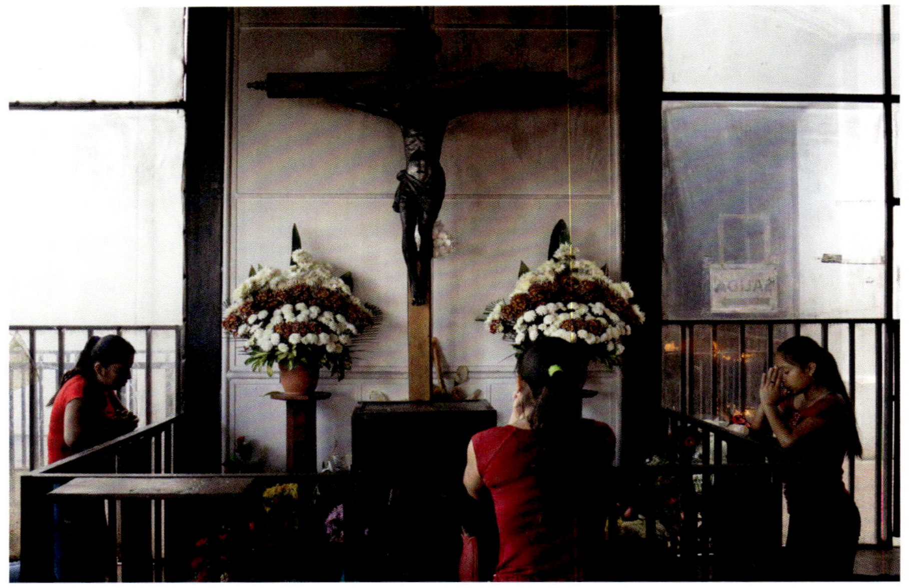

To drum up public support, Castillo Armas and Monsignor
Rossell y Arellano, the archbishop of Guatemala, turned
the Black Christ of Esquipulas into a symbol of the
anti-Communist, pro-Catholic movement.

PROGRAM SCHEDULE
FOR SEPTEMBER

ANTI-COMMUNIST	PRO-COMMUNIST
1. 32 Poster - Dios y Libertad, with cross and no. 32.	
2.	Communist statement following line of how Guatemalan Communist love Catholicism. (Handbill)
3. The Arch-Bishop's statement on Communism (Handbills).	
4. Explanation of 32 and get rid of Communism in Guatemala. (Poster)	
5. Religious poster - one with Stalin in sheep's clothing.	A Communist alert to the effect that rumors say that an attempted revolution will begin Saturday. Mobilize all forces (Handbills)
6. Stalin and the local Communist party stamping on 32 and the little people labeled "derechos", "libertad", etc.	Provide evidence of a Commie splinter group through a poster, handbill, claiming this group to be a real Nationalist "communalistic" group such as the ancient Indian population had.
7. ----------------------------------SUNDAY----------------------------------	
8. Poster ridiculing the Communist alert of the 5th.	Communist blame all trouble on the ignorance of Catholics - ridicule the Virgin of Guadelupe and quote their leaders. (Handbills)
9. List of Communist Fronts which are violating Art. 32 of their very existence and support of Communism and the USSR.	
10. Comment on the formation of the Communist splinter group.	Communists again point to immediate dangers and request a show of strength for the following day.
11. Poster showing fronts as backers of atheism and the destruction of Guatemalan liberty for the glory of - not Guatemala - but solely for the USSR.	Communist request for funds to be sent to the Soviet Embassy in Mexico, or to the Guatemalan Treasury.

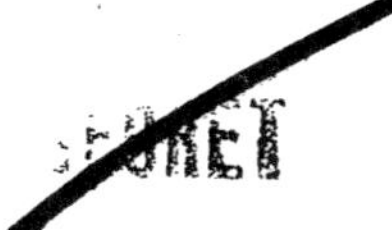

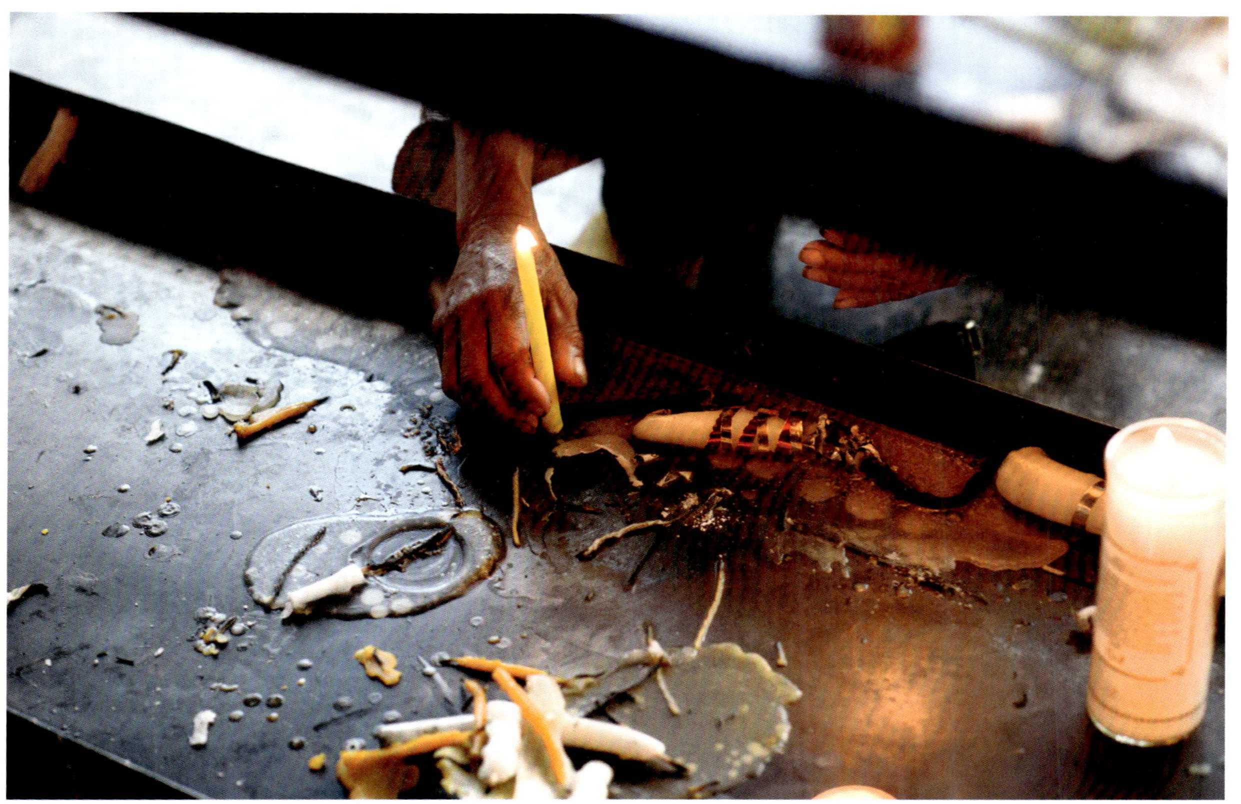

During the coup, a small army in support of Castillo Armas entered Guatemala
through Esquipulas.

The most obvious financial incentive for the coup came from the United Fruit Company (UFCO), a powerful American corporation that dominated the fruit trade in Latin America. Guatemala had been one of their earliest sites for development, and was rife with harsh working conditions, exploitation, and corruption. For years, UFCO was exempt from Guatemalan taxes and import duties. However, shortly after winning his presidency, Árbenz instituted an agrarian reform, Decree 900, that would tax UFCO while expropriating their uncultivated lands for some compensation. But UFCO had powerful allies within the United States. Allen Dulles, director of the CIA, was on its board and many elected officials had financial interests with the company. When UFCO began lobbying for support against Árbenz, the secretary of state was John Foster Dulles, Allen's brother.

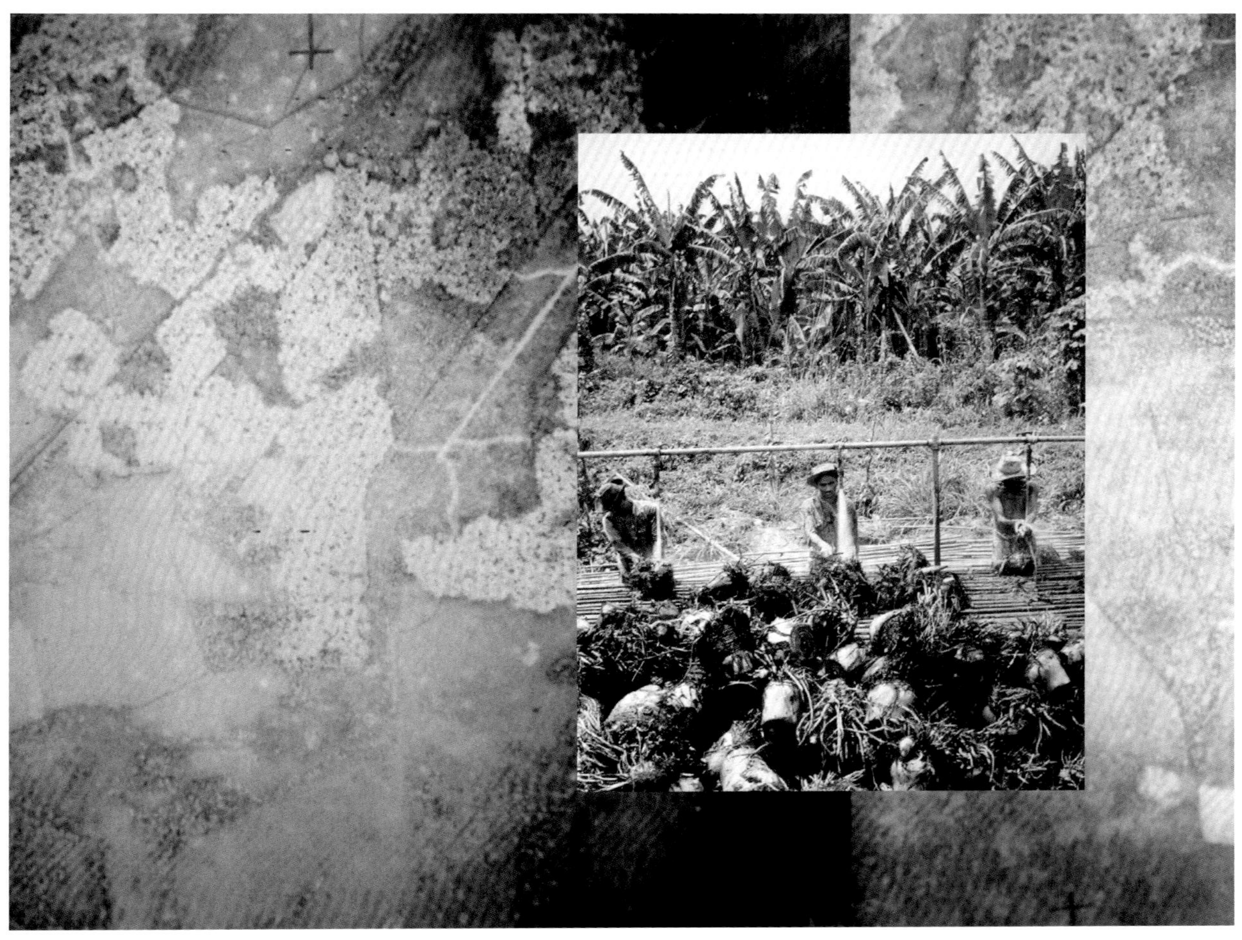

An archival photo of UFCO workers overlaid atop an aerial view of banana fincas in the 1950s.

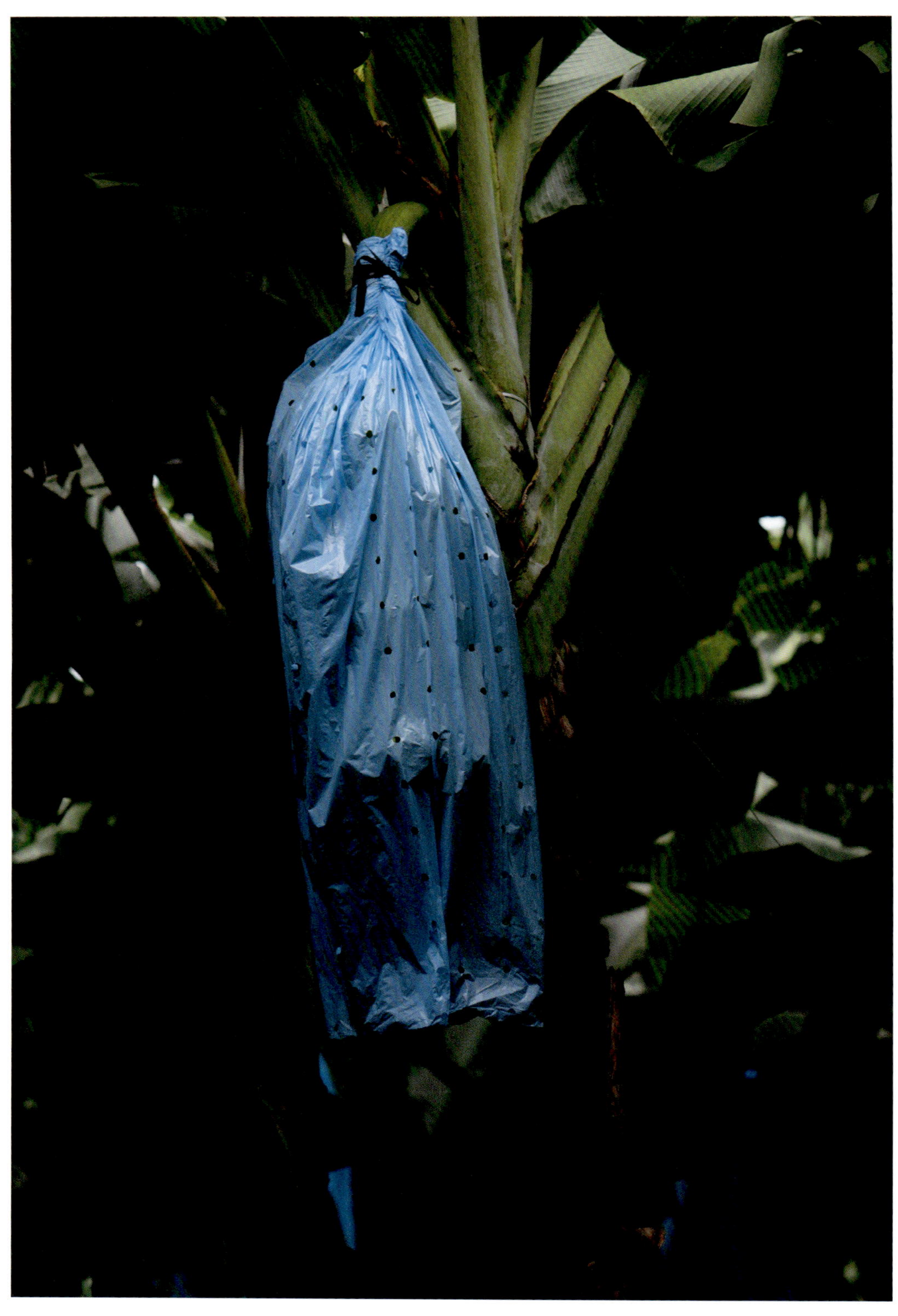

Bananas bagged for export in Puerto Barrios, Guatemala.

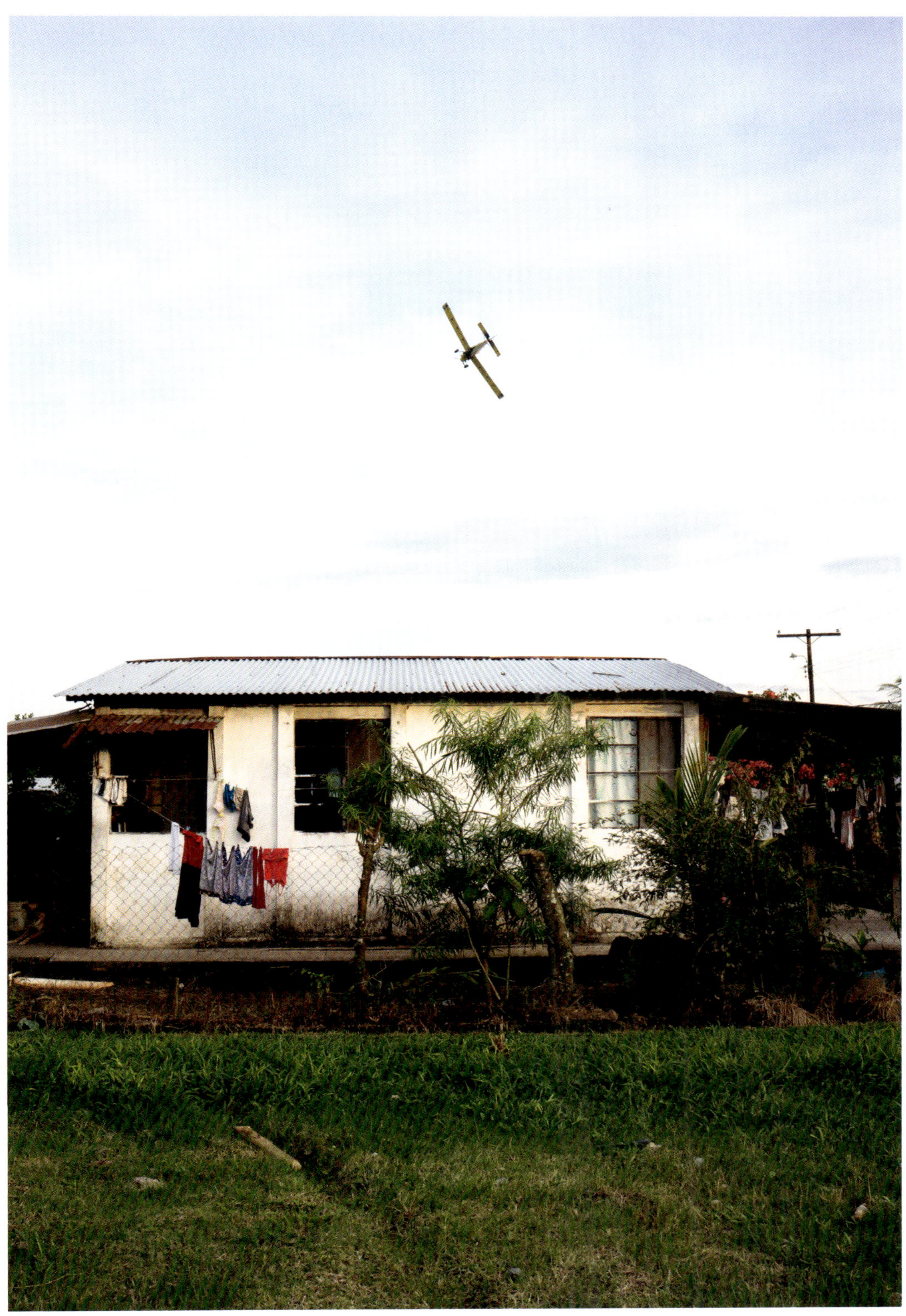

A plane sprays pesticide across the finca.

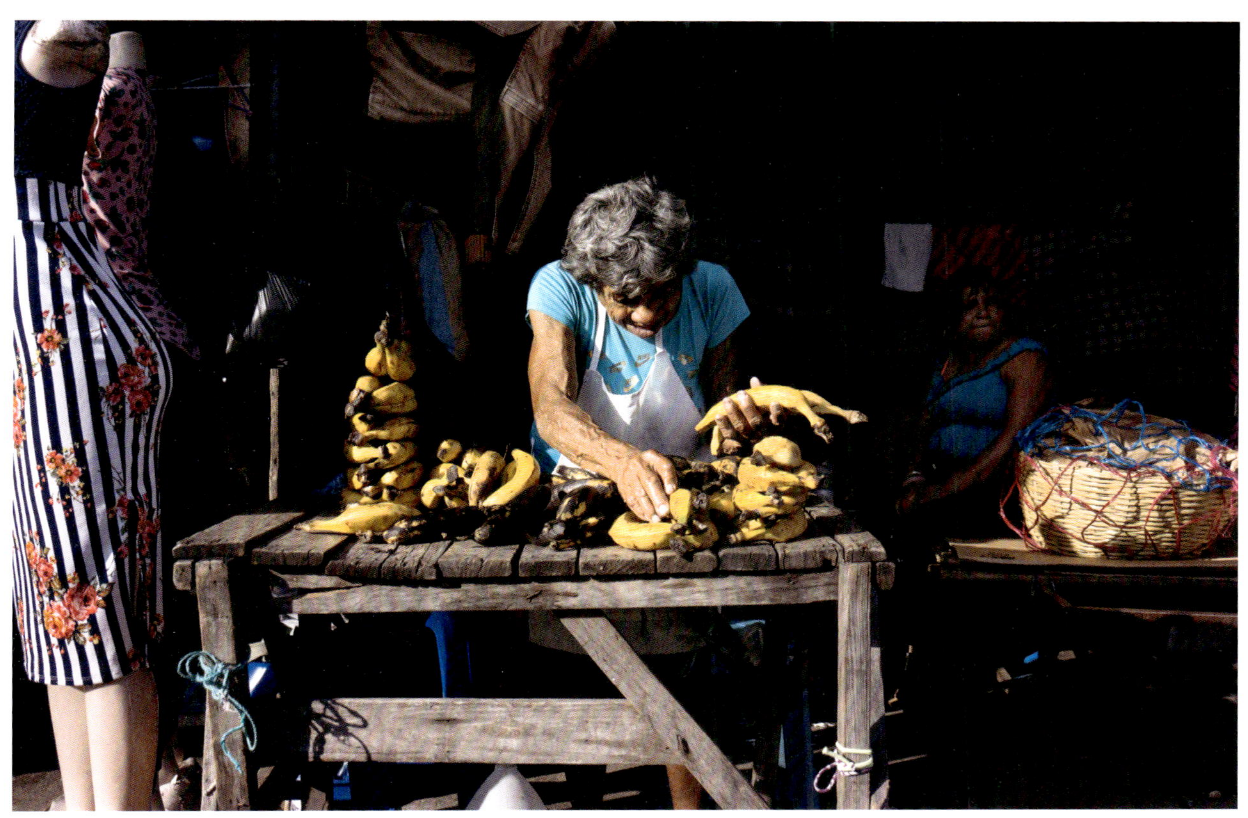

A Guatemalan vendor sells bananas that were too ripe for export.

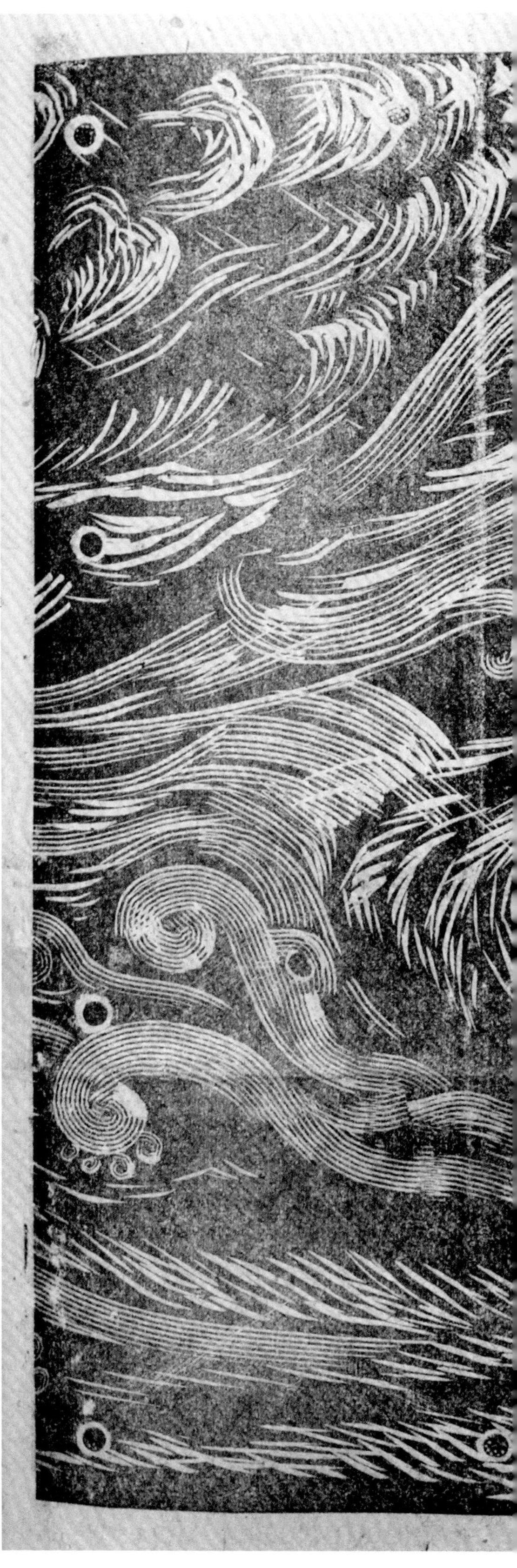

Archival drawing
depicting
banana-
plantation
laborers from
the *Diario de
Centro América*,
May 27,1954.

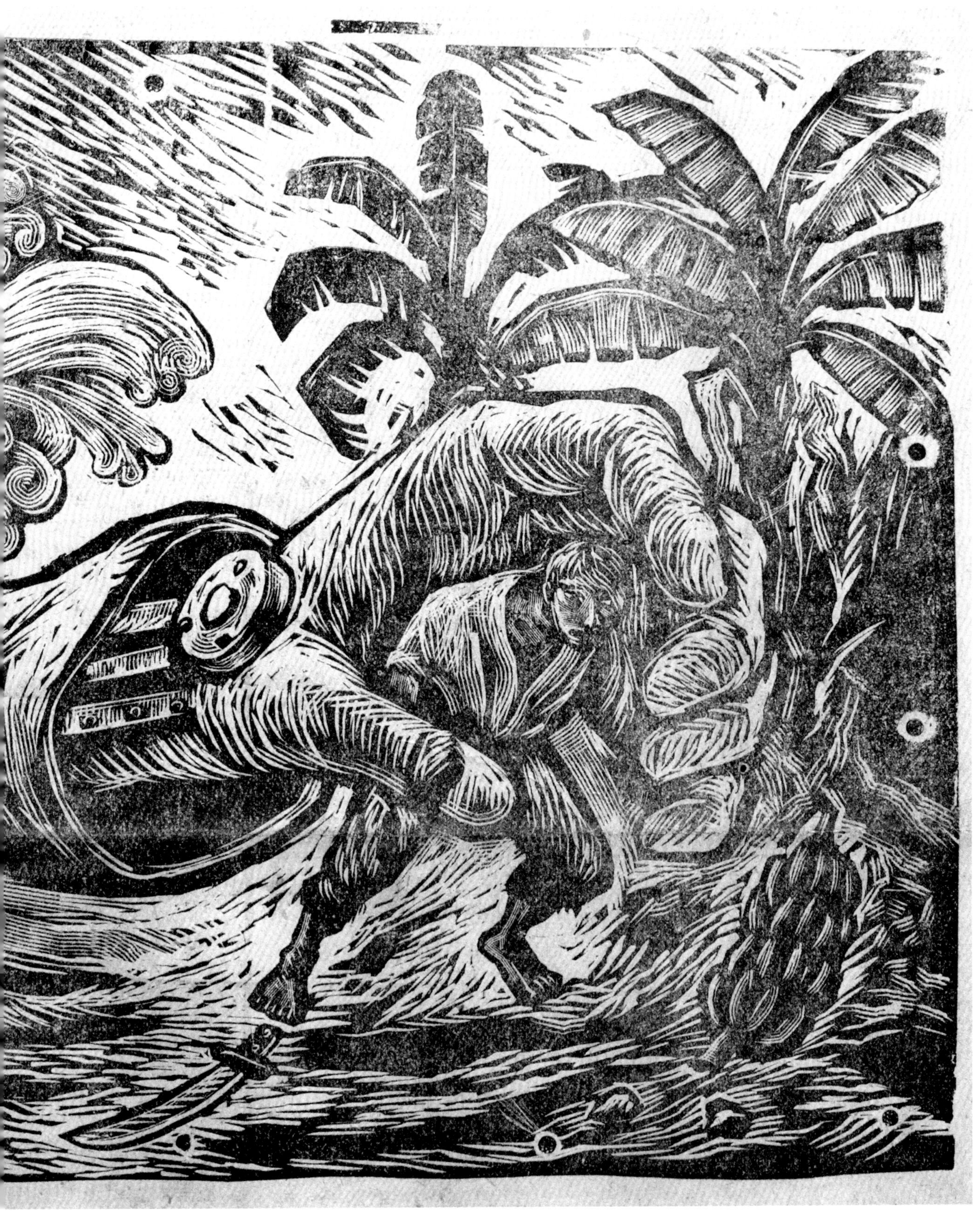

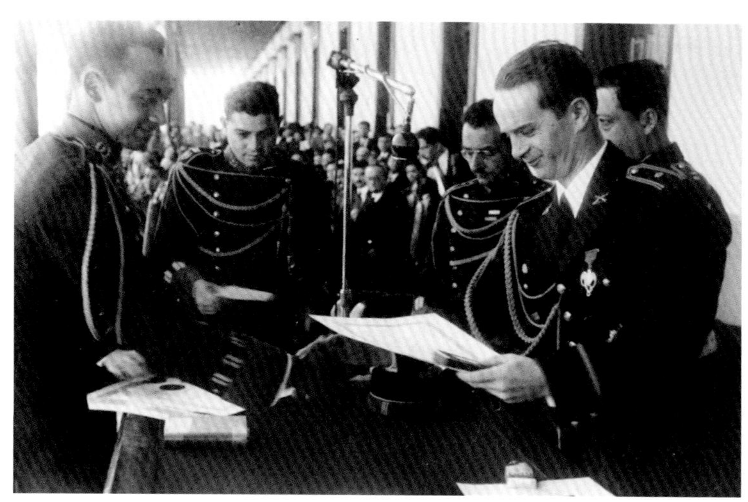

José Luis Cruz Salazar (center left) at a military ceremony with Árbenz (right). Once a friend, Cruz would end up supporting the coup against Árbenz.

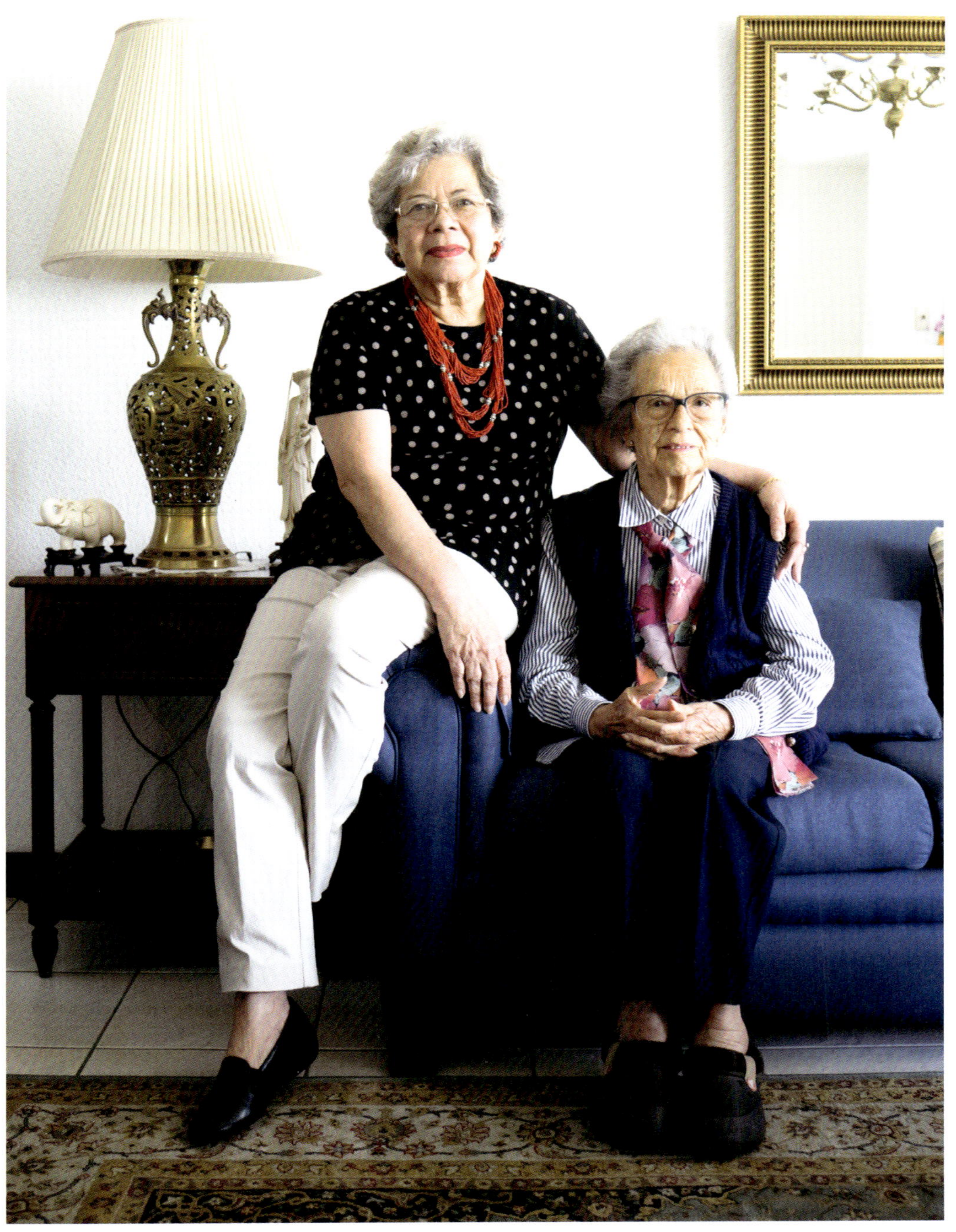

Hortensia, wife of Cruz, and her daughter, Elsie Johnston, in Guatemala City, February 2020. Under Castillo Armas's presidency, Cruz became ambassador to the United States.

"It was normal to be given parameters of what could be said in the Guatemalan newspapers.…That day, I was working as a reporter, looking on the streets for something interesting. But there was nothing to see. Everything happened behind closed doors."

—Rolando Tejada

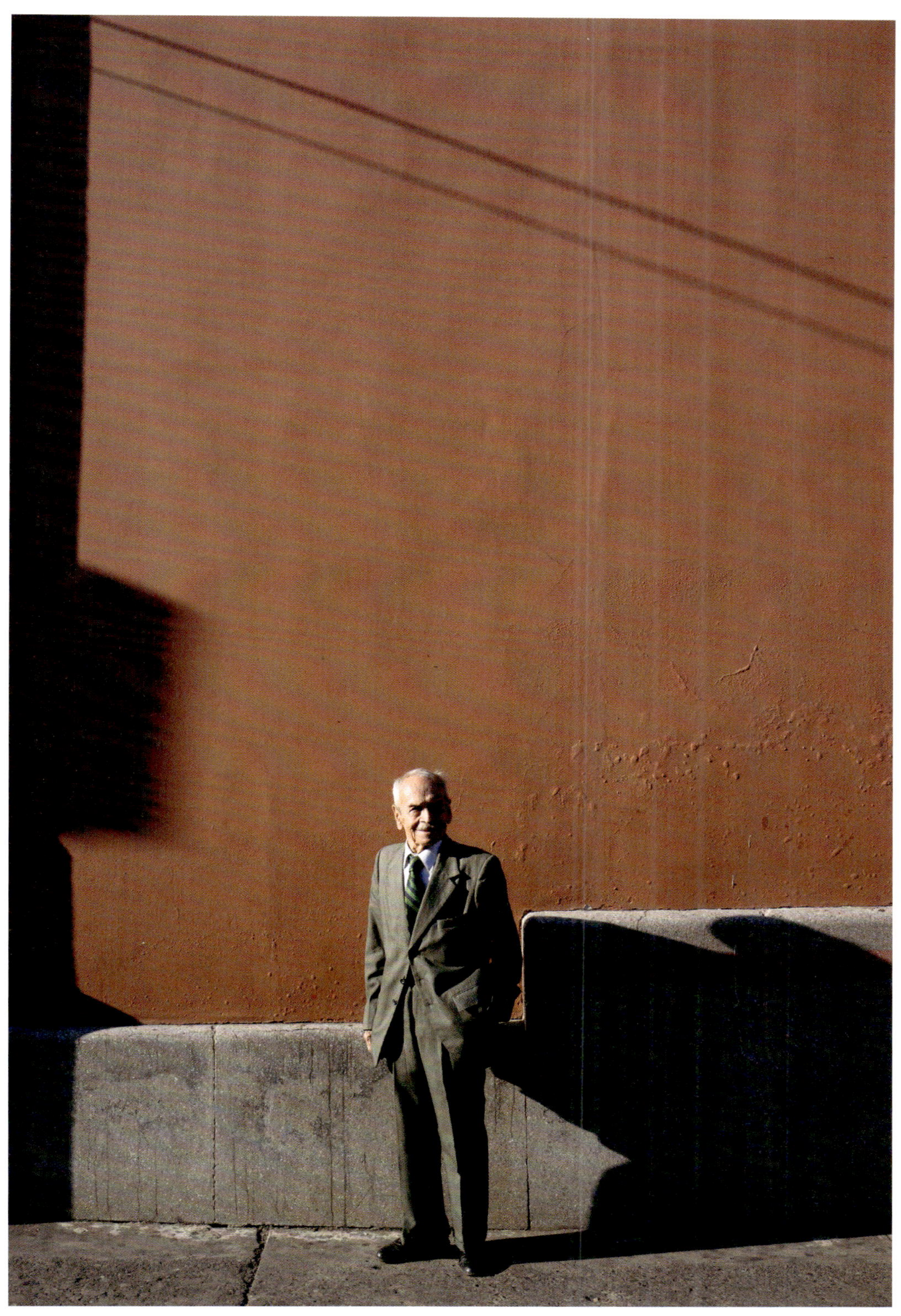

Rolando Tejada was a journalist for Guatemalan newspapers *Prensa Libre* and *El Imparcial*, at the time of the coup.

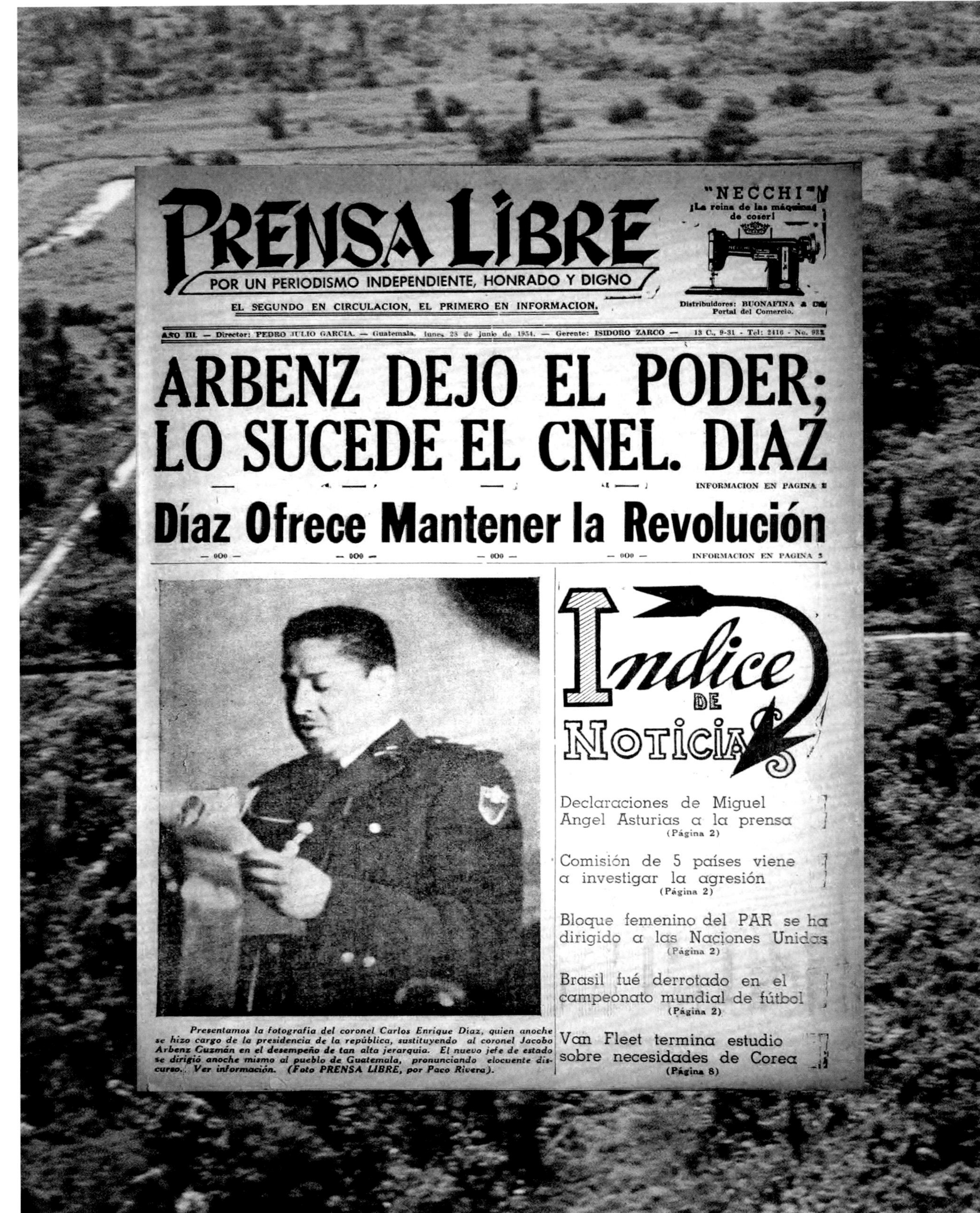

Presentamos la fotografía del coronel Carlos Enrique Díaz, quien anoche se hizo cargo de la presidencia de la república, sustituyendo al coronel Jacobo Arbenz Guzmán en el desempeño de tan alta jerarquía. El nuevo jefe de estado se dirigió anoche mismo al pueblo de Guatemala, pronunciando elocuente discurso. Ver información. (Foto PRENSA LIBRE, por Paco Rivera).

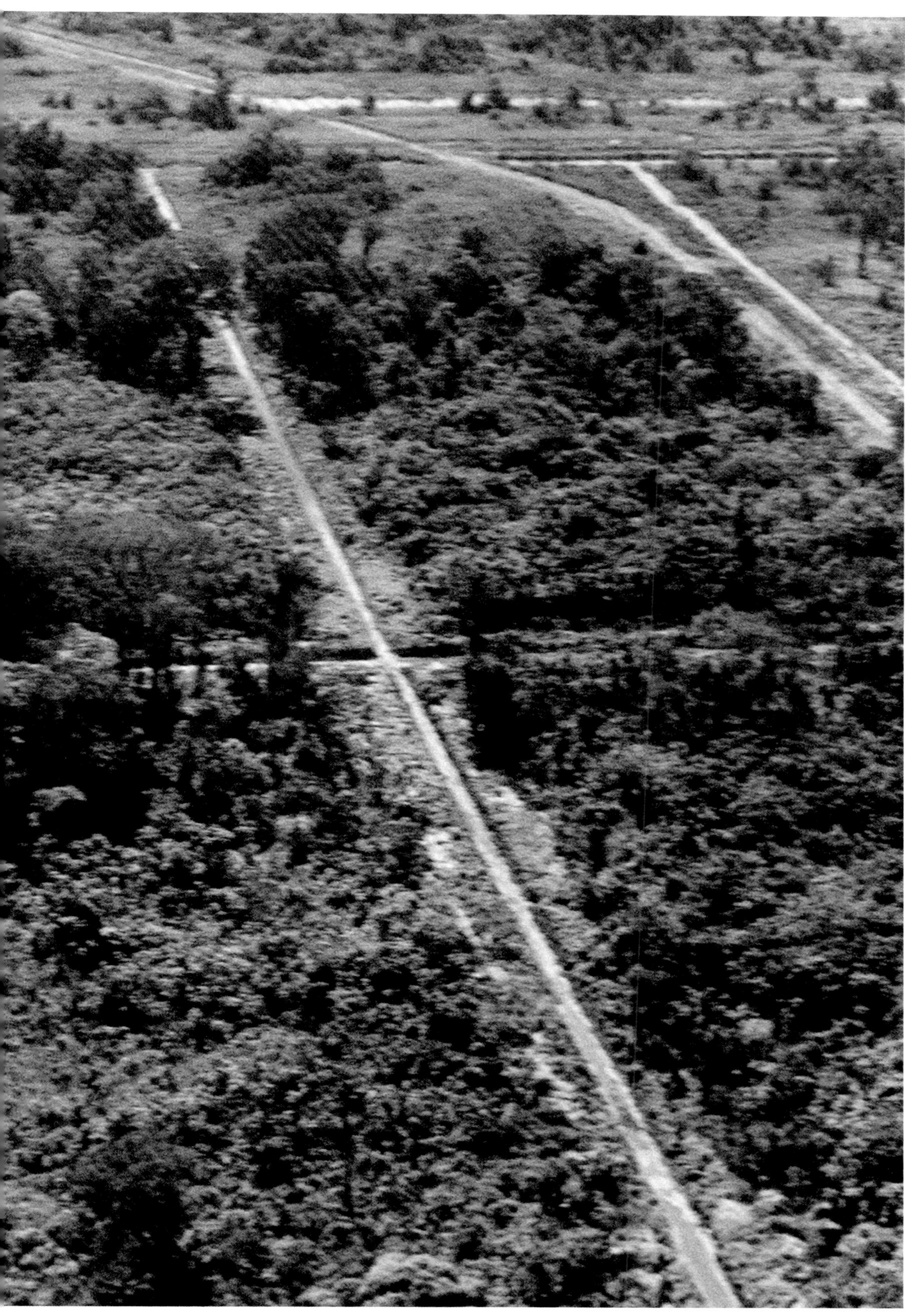

On Sunday, June 27, 1954, Árbenz was forced to resign. For weeks, the CIA had been using a radio station to wage psychological warfare, warning of uprisings and imminent war. The public was on edge. The military had withdrawn its support and many of his allies had fled. Members of his own administration, some of whom had been friends from the military academy, were siding with the United States.

For one day, Coronel Carlos Enrique Díaz de León, a former supporter of Árbenz, assumed power, but the US had no intention of having him lead. He was forcibly removed overnight. Three different military juntas followed, each with members who'd been paid by the CIA, until Castillo Armas was officially named president four months later. According to my family, Castillo Armas was my grandfather's personal choice. His superiors had wanted someone more conservative.

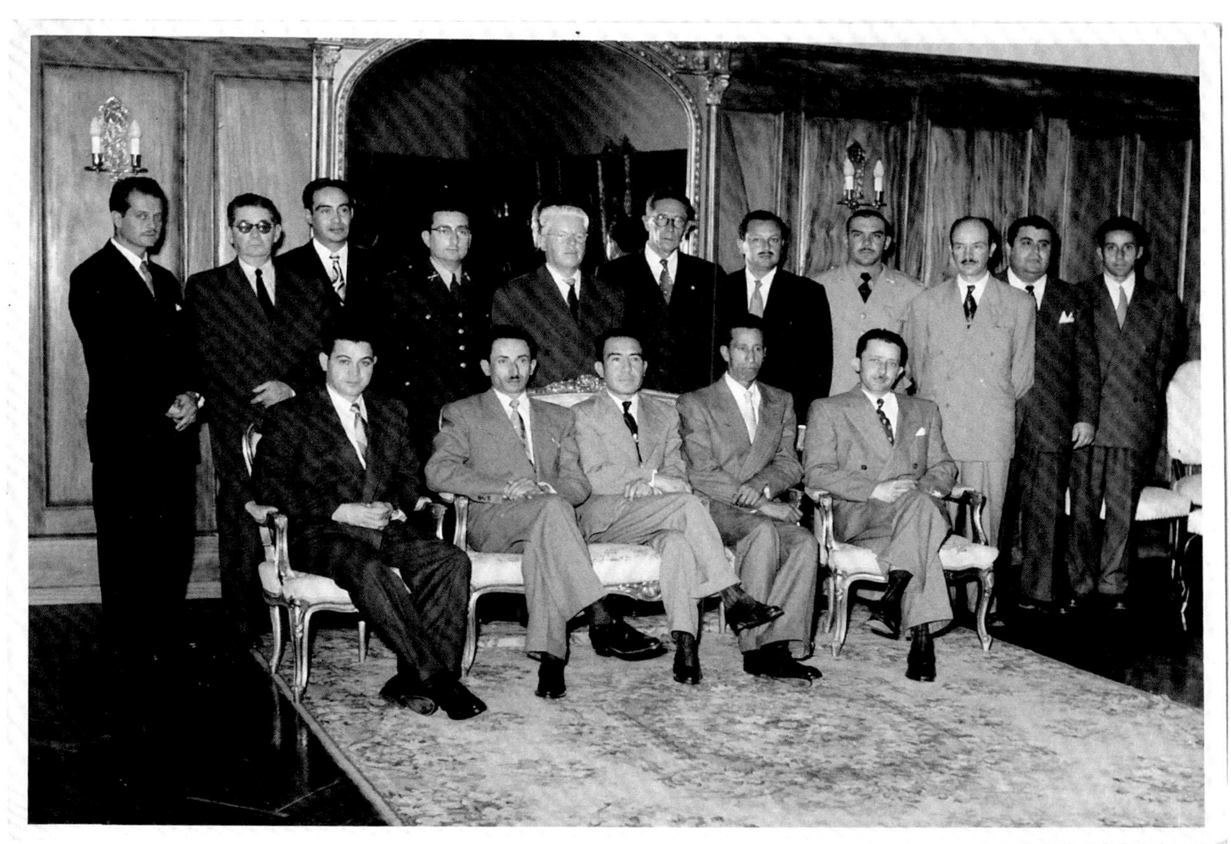

Members of the second military junta and associates. The junta, seated in the first row, from left: José Luis Cruz Salazar, Castillo Armas, Elfego Monzón Aguirre, Enrique Trinidad Oliva, Mauricio Dubois.

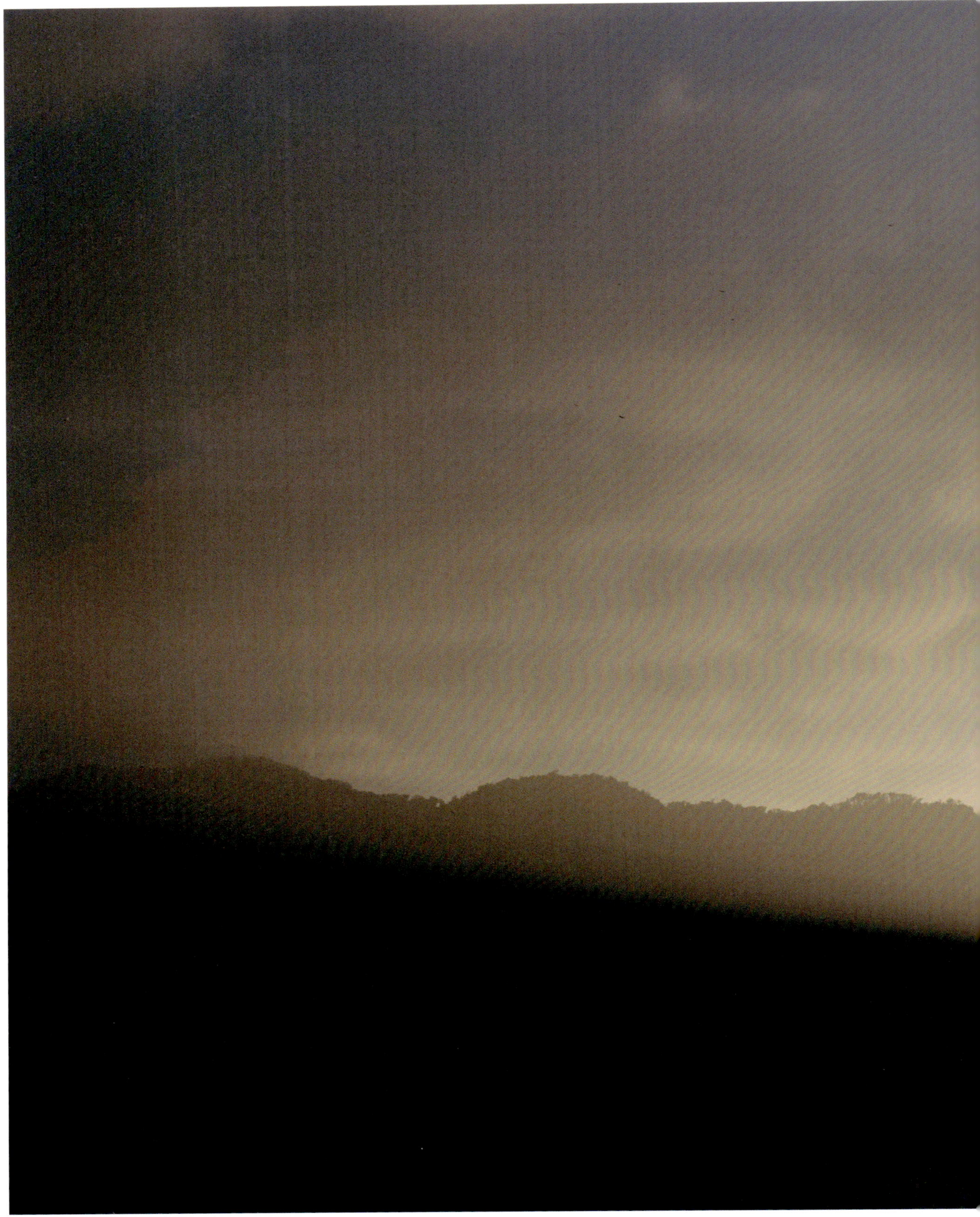

Working in Guatemala was like navigating a multidimensional web without a beginning or an end. Every conversation was layered. Nothing was exactly as it seemed. History had become more polarized over time, and now sharply different realities existed. At its core, there were facts that I believed wholeheartedly: the CIA had unjustly intervened and put in place a series of increasingly violent and dogmatic dictators. But I interviewed people with starkly different personal histories. People who only spoke to me because my grandfather was John Dougherty. Instead of being insightful, I found it disorienting, almost nauseating, as though I was working under a constant state of vertigo. It was the beginning of 2019 and the same kind of revisionist history that I was experiencing in Guatemala had gathered steam in the United States. I wondered if we had become victims of our own methods of psychological warfare.

"Árbenz was openly left-wing. Not only left-wing, but a dictator…he armed many civilians. He put in their heads, 'You're going to get rich if we do this.'" Then he got support from many people in the rural areas. Those armed people were the ones who came and enforced the agrarian reform, and they took my grandfather's farm. They burned all those acres of sugarcane."

—Marta Altolaguirre Larraondo

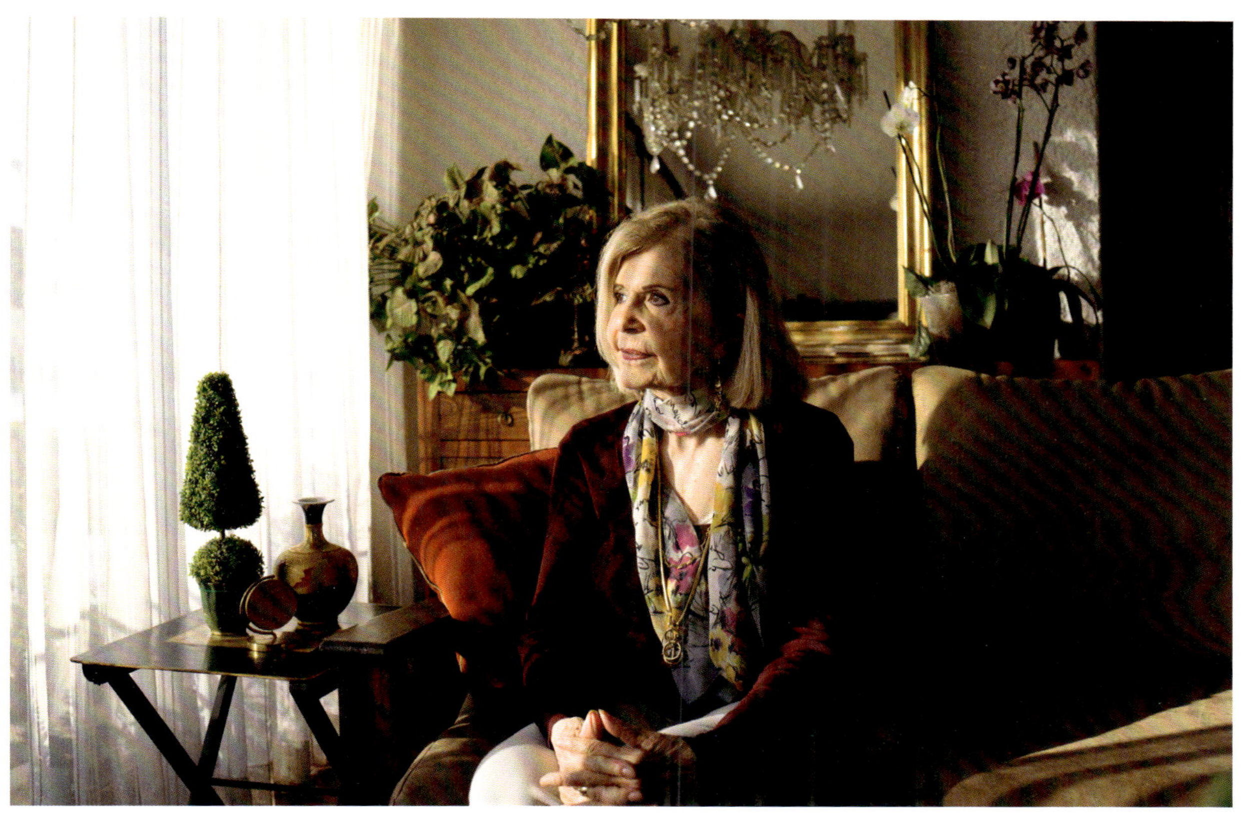

Marta Altolaguirre Larraondo is the former vice minister of Foreign Affairs and a lawyer who helped broker the 1996 peace accords. Guatemala City, October 2019.

Right: José Antonio Móbil Beltetón was the leader of the San Carlos Student Association (AEU), a leftist revolutionary organization that supported Árbenz. The group continued to operate for five years after the coup until many of its members were forced into exile. Guatemala City, August 2019.

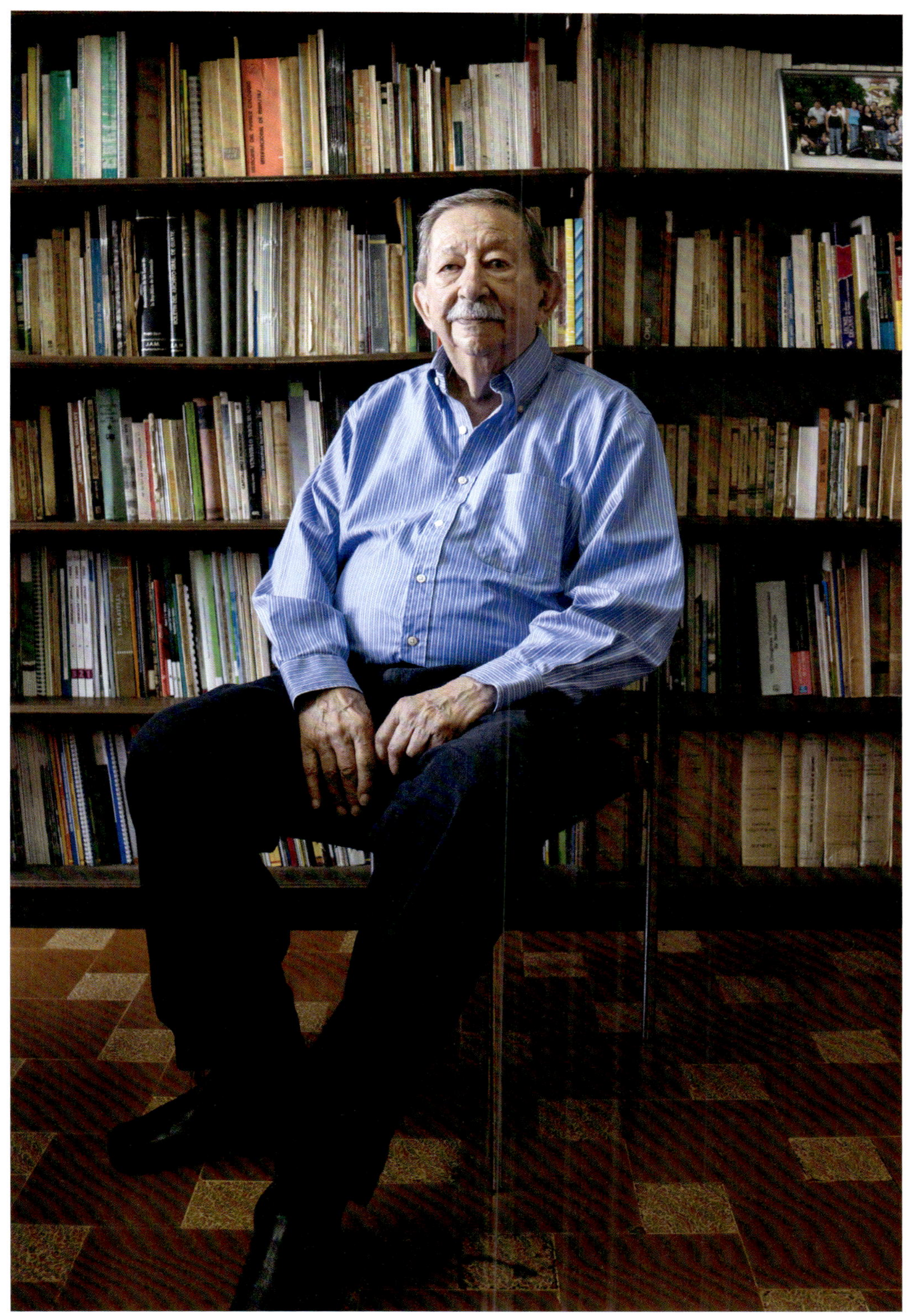

*"There are thousands
of such stories. There is
a bias in the reporting
about what happened [in
'54]. There was no coup.
That is another mistake.
It was a collapse. The
collapse of a giant."*

—Augusto de León Fajardo

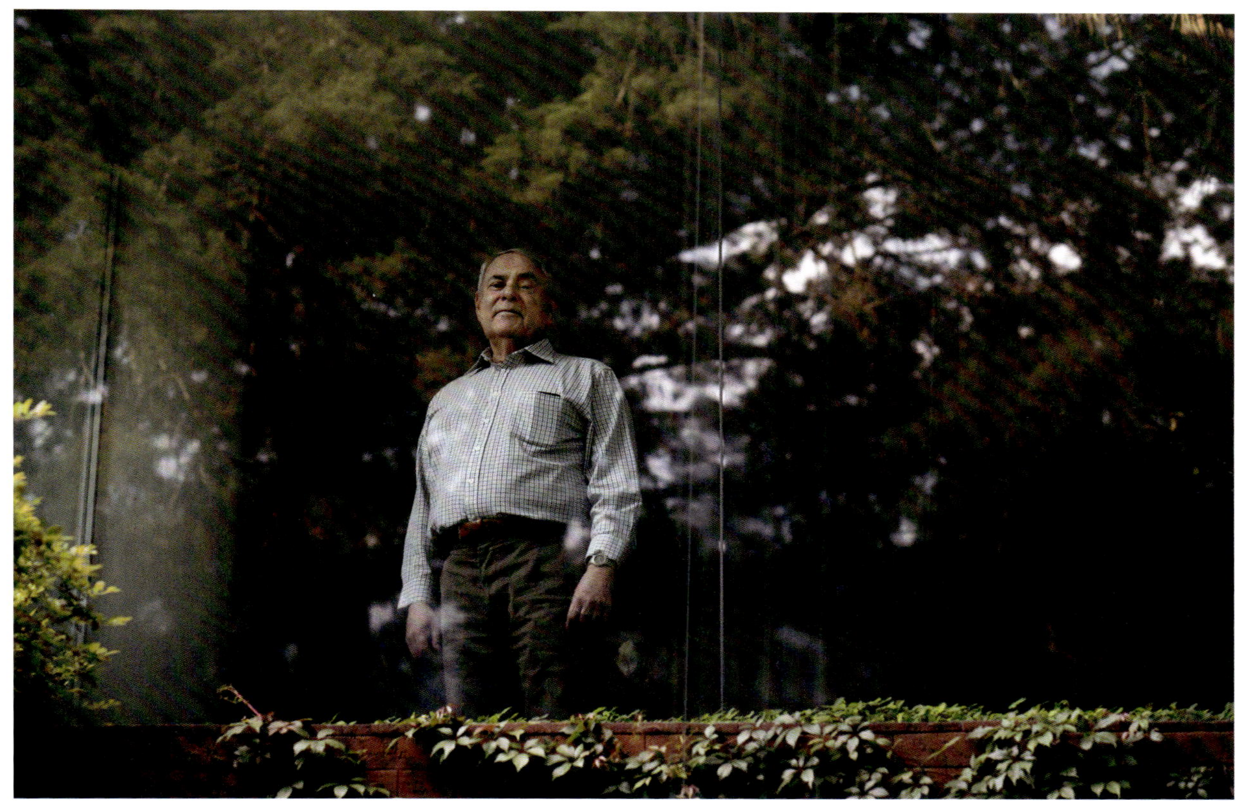

Augusto de León Fajardo's father, Romeo, was vice president of Congress in 1966 when he was kidnapped by the revolutionary guerrillas that opposed the right-wing, army-dominated administration. He has spoken out against the reported captures of anti-Communists during the Árbenz presidency and afterwards by the guerrillas.

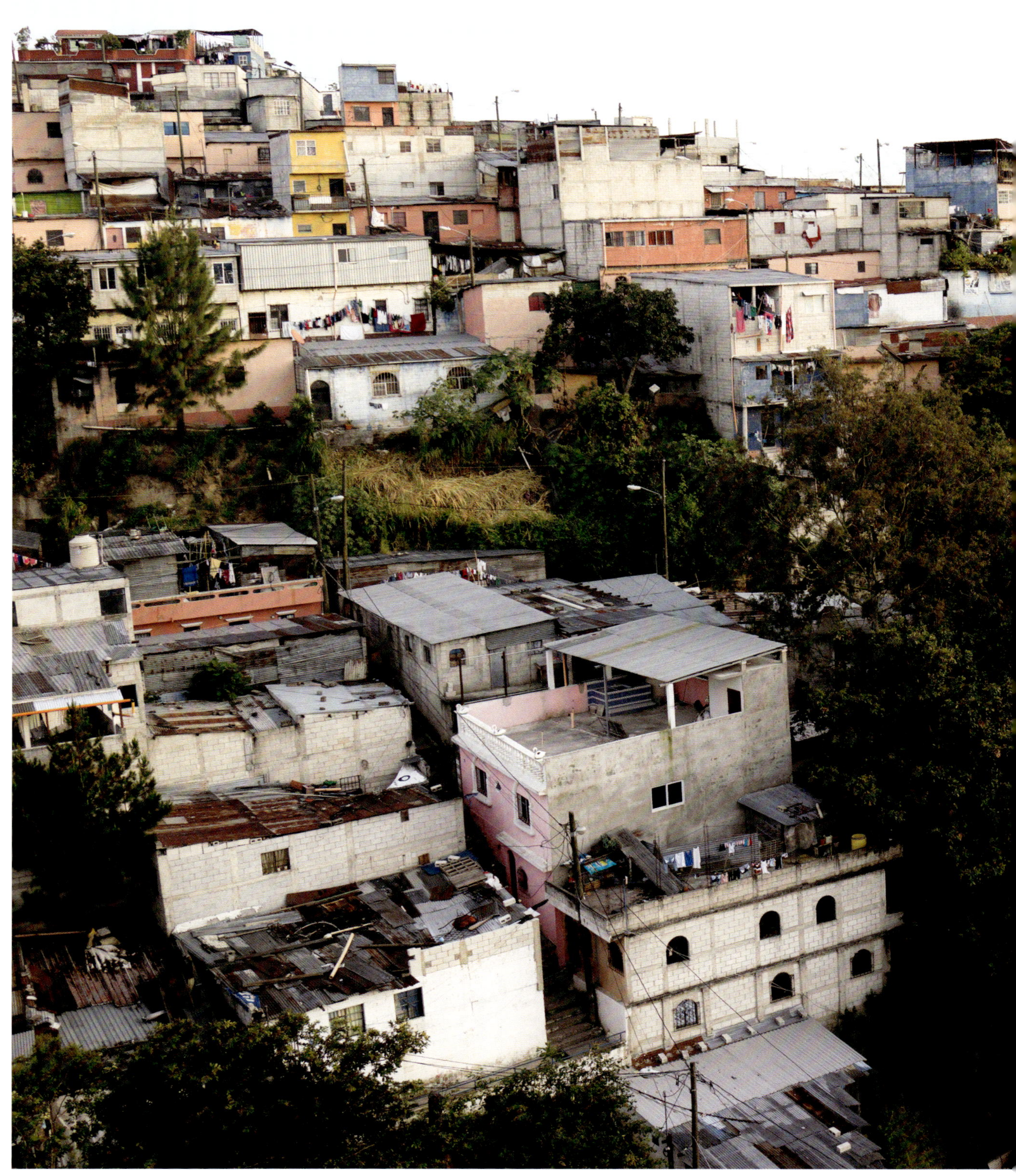

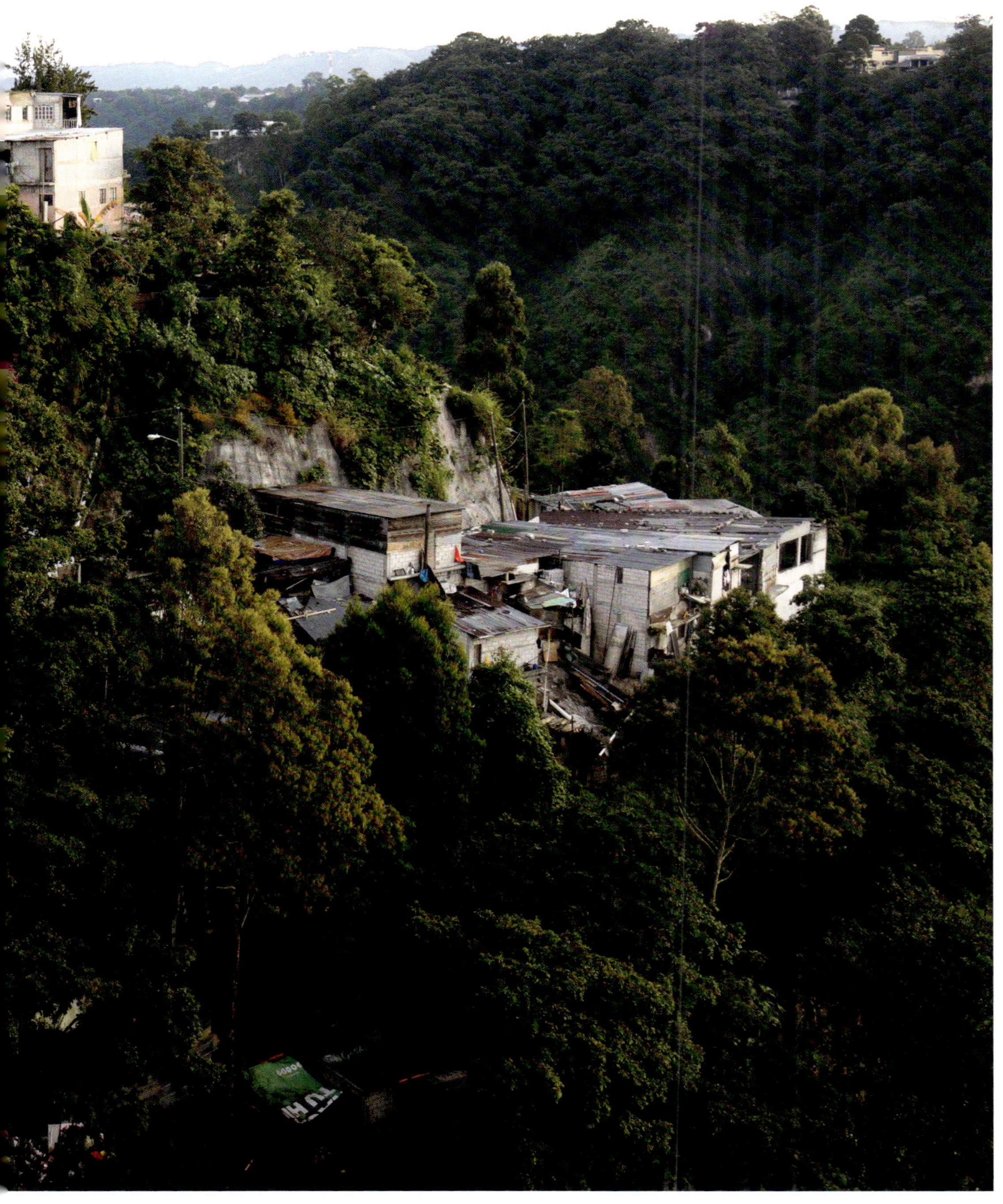

"I'm going to tell you something very important, now that you tell me that your grandfather was involved in the CIA…and you can't say that I am one of those intolerable landowners; I'm not. How much does it cost people to maintain a property? Families cultivate the land, particularly coffee and cotton. It's been inherited and learned. But what these Communists wanted was to distribute the land. For what? So that they would sow corn. How could they lift people out of poverty who knew absolutely nothing?"

—Héctor Menéndez

Right: Héctor Menéndez, whose father worked for Castillo Armas's administration after the coup. It's likely that he worked alongside my grandfather. In 1963, he was kidnapped by guerrillas alongside Romeo.

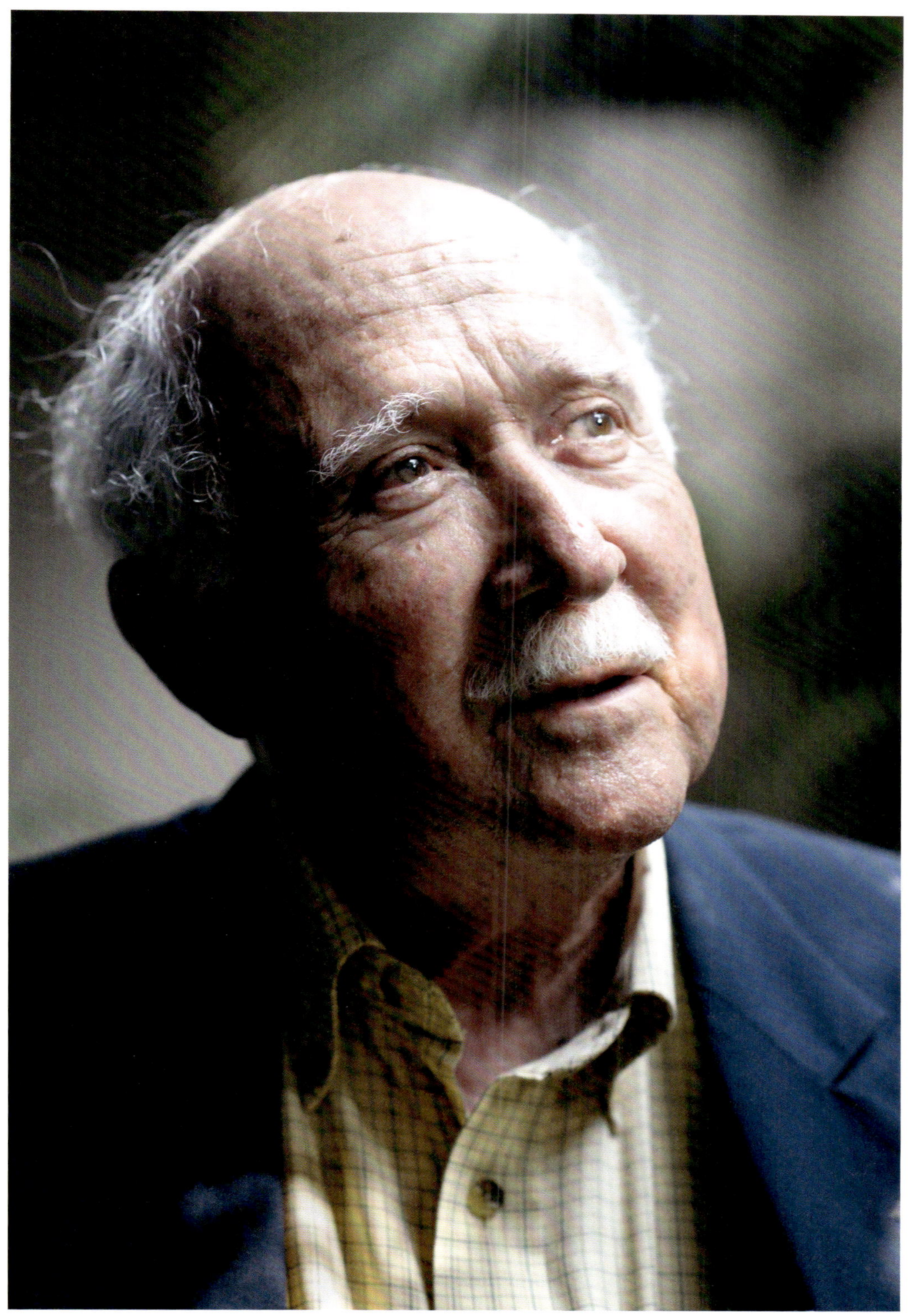

*"We left because the
US wanted to kill
the Communists."*
—Luis Felipe Sánchez

PRENSA LIBRE

POR UN PERIODISMO INDEPENDIENTE, HONRADO Y DIGNO

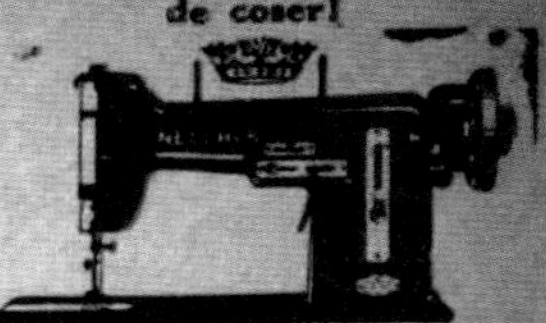

EL SEGUNDO EN CIRCULACION,   EL PRIMERO EN INFORMACION.

AÑO III. — Director: PEDRO JULIO GARCIA. — Guatemala, viernes 2 de julio de 1954. — Gerente: ISIDORO ZARCO. — 13 C., 9-31 - Tel: 2416 - No. 927

¡Pacto de Paz! Castillo Armas y Monzón logran pleno acuerdo

Más de 400 Comunistas Capturados

INFORMACION EN PAGINA 4

LISTA COMPLETA DE ROJOS EN LA JUDICIAL

INFORMACION EN PAGINA 3

CASTILLO ARMAS Y OLIVA SE INCORPORAN A JUNTA DE GOB.

A las dos horas y treinta minutos de hoy, en la casa presidencial de la hermana república de El Salvador, se firmó el pacto de paz entre el coronel Carlos Castillo Armas, jefe del ejército de la liberación y el coronel Elfego H. Monzón, presidente de la junta de gobierno, con lo cual se llega al triunfo final en la lucha emprendida para librar por completo a Guatemala del comunismo.

En ese histórico acto estuvieron presentes además de los coroneles mencionados, el señor Carlos Azúcar Chávez, jefe del protocolo, en representación del presidente Oscar Osorio; el embajador de los Estados Unidos en Guatemala, señor John E. Peurifoy; el embajador de El Salvador en Guatemala, coronel José Alberto Funes, el nuncio apostólico del Vaticano en Centro América, monseñor Genaro Verolino y algunos funcionarios del gobierno salvadoreños. Todos los nombrados en las líneas anteriores actuaron como mediadores en los caminos hacia la paz.

Entre las cuestiones fundamentales resueltas en "el pacto de San Salvador" está la integración de una nueva junta de gobierno, identificados todos sus miembros en la lucha contra el comunismo y la cual quedó así: coronel Elfego H. Monzón, teniente coronel Carlos Castillo Armas, teniente coronel Juan Mauricio Dubois, teniente coronel José Luis Cruz Salazar y coronel Enrique Oliva, quienes tomarán posesión de sus cargos inmediatamente.

Al referirse a tan importante como patriótico acontecimiento, el coronel Carlos Castillo Armas, enfocó la trascendencia del mismo para el bienestar de Guatemala e hizo profesión de fe en un futuro democrático y de paz interna. El coronel Monzón, jefe de la junta de gobierno, dijo que "Nuestros ideales y propósitos, están encaminados a formar una sola unidad".

El pacto en cuestión, que consta de doce puntos, fué firmado por los coroneles Castillo Armas y Monzón y las distinguidas personas que actuaron como mediadoras.

Entre los aspectos básicos del "pacto" figura el cese total de hostilidades; que el ejército de liberación se incorpora al ejército nacional en plena identificación ideológica; que el coronel Elfego Monzón, será el presidente provisional de la junta por un plazo no mayor de quince días, después de los cuales entre todos los integrantes de la propia junta se procederá a elegir al presidente definitivo; que se convocará a elecciones presidenciales; que se llamará a una constituyente; la nueva procederá a integrar el poder judicial.

Uno de los detenidos en Salamá por las autoridades arbencistas muestra cómo le dejaron la espalda sus verdugos para arrancarle confesiones para el fal...

No pague más de 5 centavos

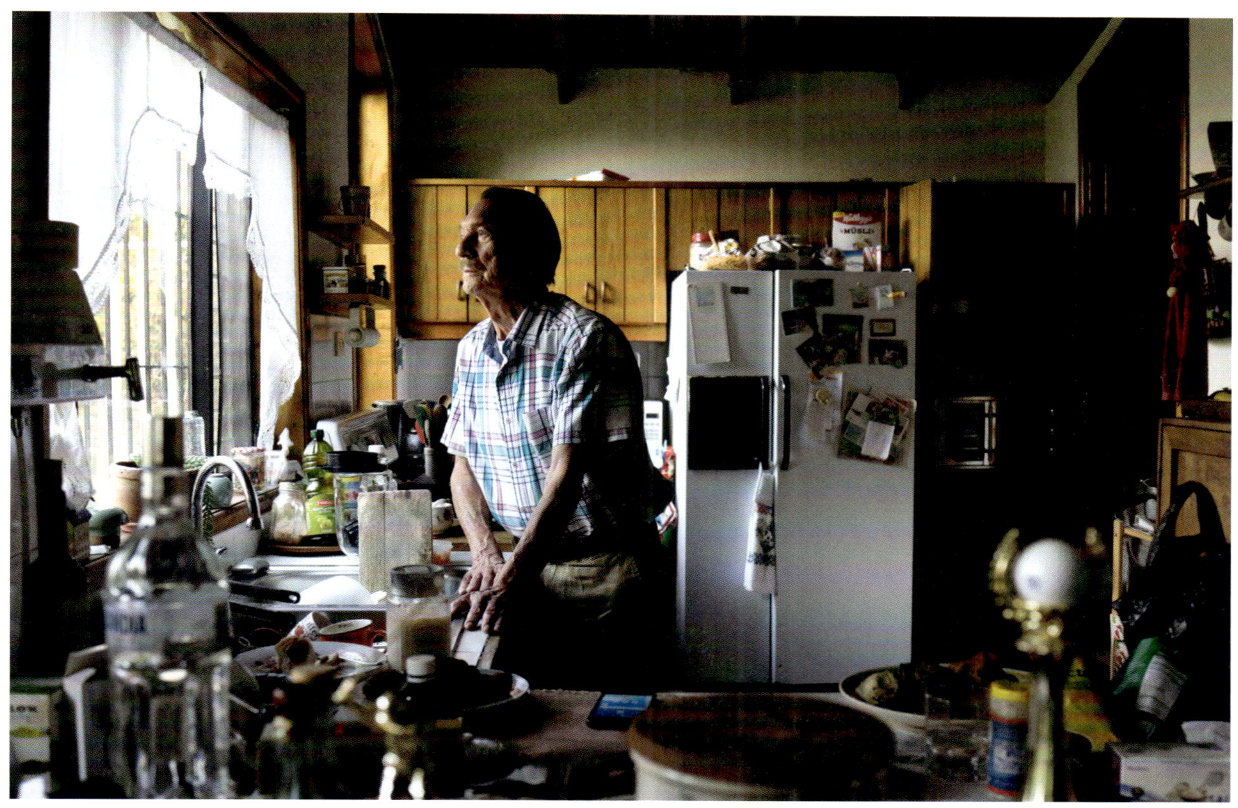

Luis Felipe Sánchez's father, José, was the minister of defense for Árbenz. After the coup, José joined one of the military juntas, but according to Luis, he didn't identify with the right-wing movement or the left. With seemingly no middle ground left, he and his family left Guatemala for seven years.

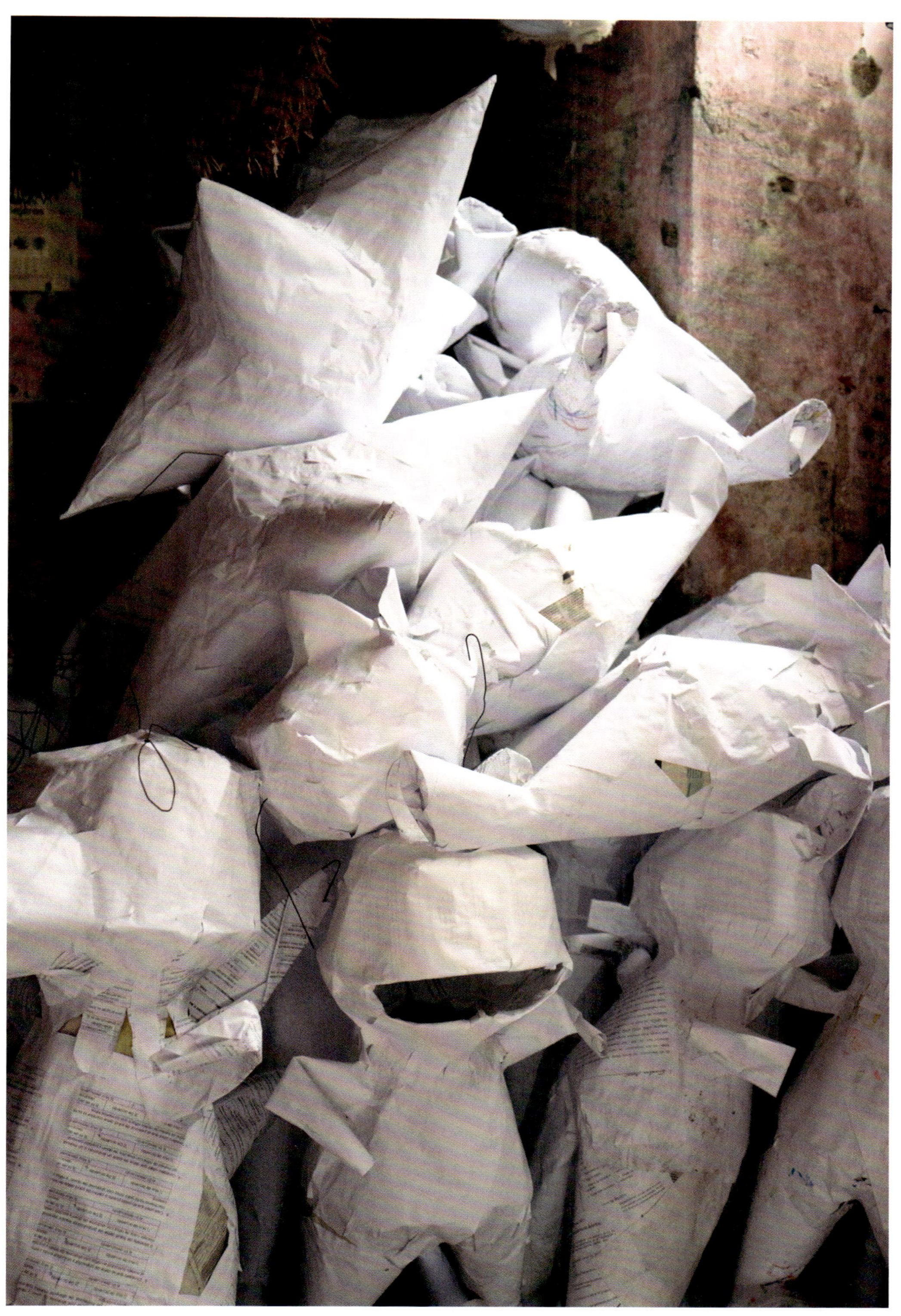

Guatemala City, 2019.

Cable: **RADAM** - Dirección: 3a. C. 8-31, Zona 1 - Teléfonos: 27814 - 29312
Radam

RADIO AMERICA, S. A.

GUATEMALA, GUATEMALA, C. A.

Dearest Jo: Wednesday, 30 August.

Day after day goes by and with each day I hope that I am closer to a
solution of this horrible and thorney situation. I hasten to say that from the
legal standpoint it is not so horrible or so thorney (or is it thorny?) but there
are so many things that I have to settle that I do not know just where I stand.

I wonder if you received two hundred dollars from Miss Kimball, Kidd
of Miami ██
██
██
██

At this time I am trying to collect and arrange things so that I shall
have some ██
██
██
██
████████████████████████ you all so terribly that I hardly know what to do. Incidently,
Helen is leaving today for the States, She has to go to Johns Hopkins f█████
██

I now have Enrique dead to rights and it looks as though he will get
██
██
██
██
██

I seem to be running around on a treadmill and not really accomplishing
much of anything although I am assured that all goes well. My insoluble problem
up to the present time is that of money. We just have not been able to collect.
I am constantly pushing this matter and I ████████████████████████████████████
within the next couple of days. If at ███████████████████████████████████████
██
██
the hand I have been doing in writing from one day to another in the hope that
██

I find it so hard to write since I have so little to tell you that is
definite. This lack of accomplishment is driving me to distraction and I am afraid
that my disposition is suffering badly from it all.

I am so anxious to see and to talk to you and to be with you and with
the children that I hardly can contain myself. God grant that this be FAST. One
thing for sure, If I do not manage to get up by Saturday or Sunday, I shall send
you what funds I can by cable. However, I do believe that I shall make it by the n.
Perhaps I shall phone you tonight. I am so desperate to hear your voice.

With all my love to you and to the children. And I do love you!

Shortly after the coup, my grandfather quit the CIA. He believed he was being set up as the scapegoat for the internationally criticized operation. When they tried to demote him, he quit, staying in Guatemala to start several businesses that leveraged the connections he'd made as an officer. He loved the country and believed that his businesses could help stabilize the economy. But staying was his foray into a more volatile side of Guatemala, one without the protections afforded to a CIA station chief. Why he took this risk is a question that my mom and I can't answer. Or maybe we can; we just don't want to believe that he could be that stubborn, that his interests could have clouded the very judgment he spent years honing. For every powerful connection he'd made, there were just as many enemies. Now those enemies included the CIA, who he believed were tracking him. They thought he'd been compromised.

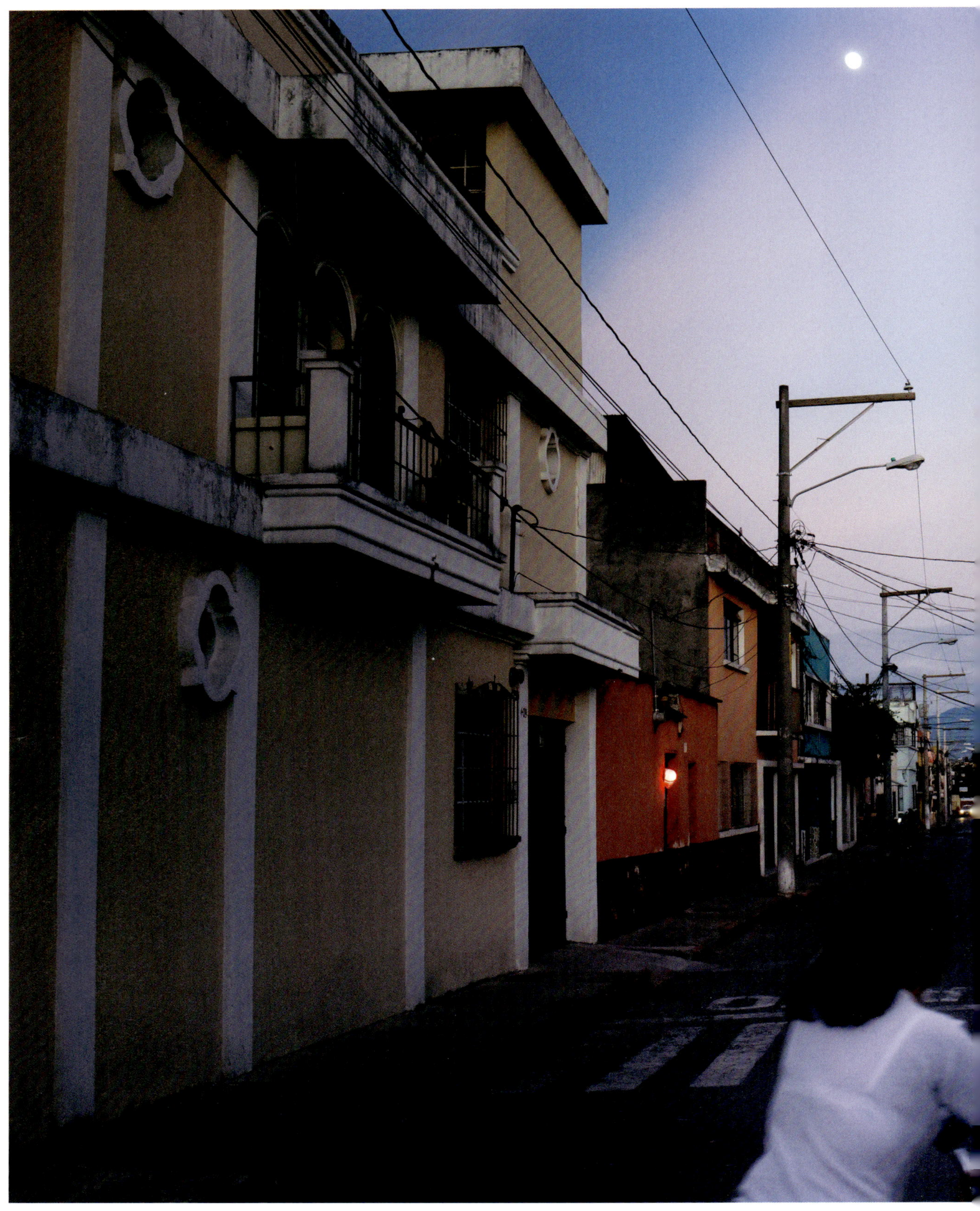

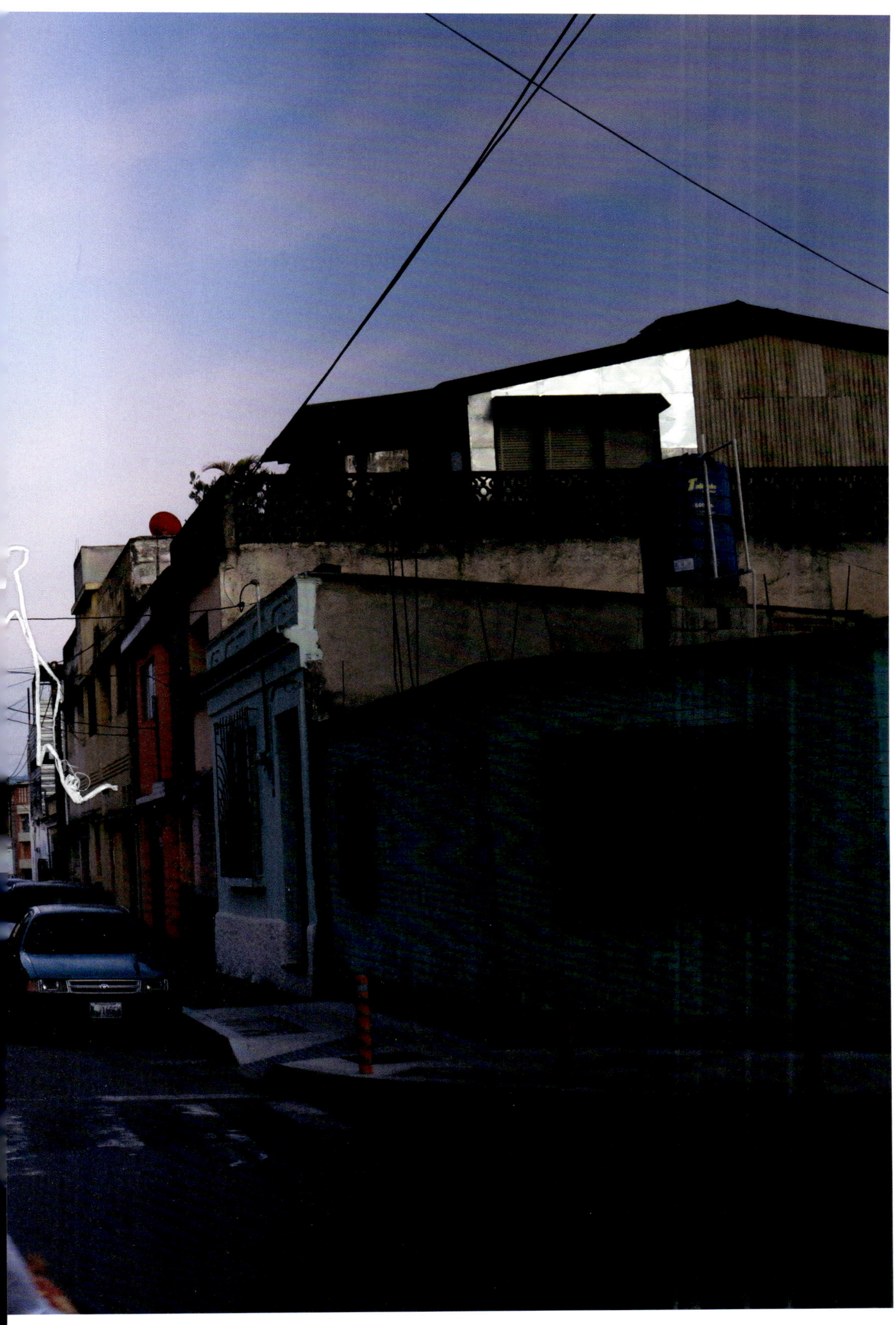

Current Political Atmosphere

Mr. Mann described Guatemala politics as an incredible maze of intrigue, fathered by ignorance, inexperience, and native suspicion. He cited the example of Clemente Marroquin Rojas' attack on Mr. Mann for allegedly recommending his expulsion. The Embassy had learned that the story came from inside the palace, where someone was busily adding to the thick layer of lies and rumors which covered the city, and which holds up the business which has to be transacted. President Castillo trusts no one, and seems to believe the last man who has spoken to him, in many cases. Not even his own cabinet ministers can be informed of matters discussed by the President with the Embassy. A further complication is the presence of John Dougherty, who has the President's ear. The Embassy believed he was misleading the President, ... Jerry DeLarm was apparently lying low, for the time being, at least. His was strictly a problem of money....

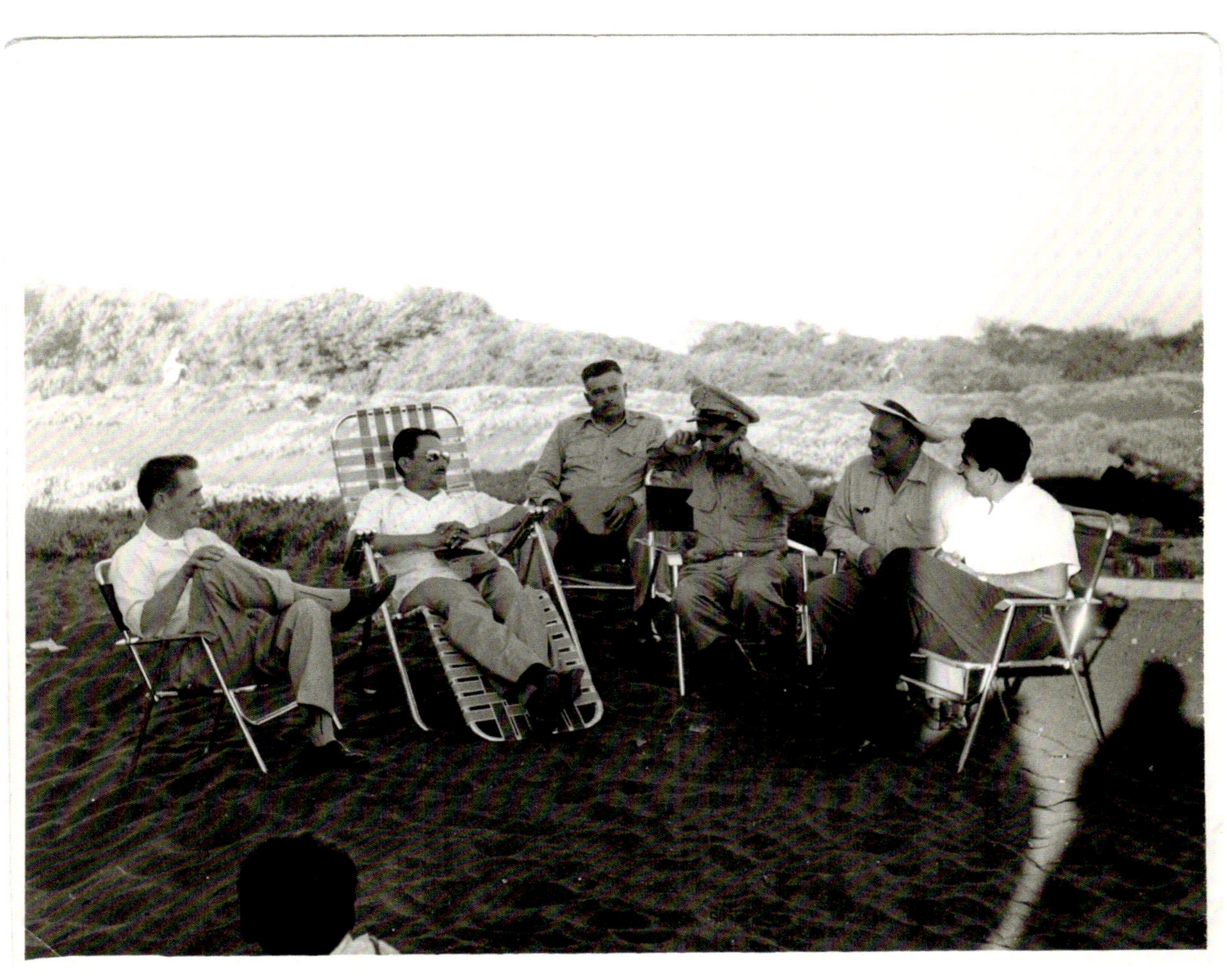

John, my grandfather (left); Castillo Armas (center left); members of the infamous MLN army and Mario Sandoval (right), who would soon lead the MLN as they operated as a death squad. The photo was taken sometime around 1956. By then, my grandfather had already quit the CIA.

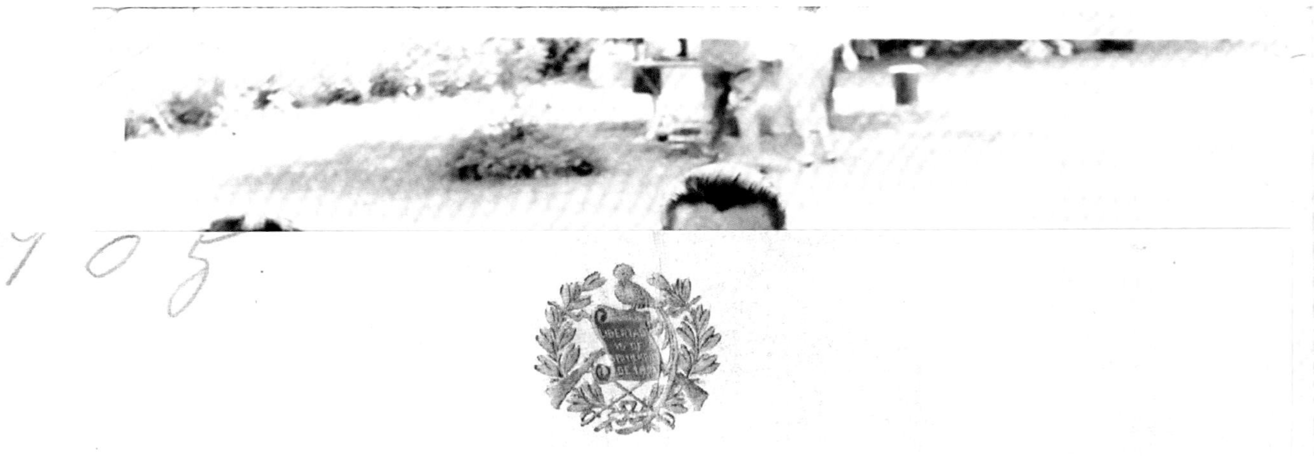

El Presidente de la República
y la Señora de Castillo Armas

se complacen en invitar a usted a la Recepción que, en conmemoración del CXXXIV Aniversario de la Independencia Patria, ofrecerán en el Salón de Recepciones del Palacio Nacional, el jueves 15 del mes en curso, de las 18:30 a las 20:00 horas.

Guatemala, septiembre de 1955.

TRAJE: OBSCURO.

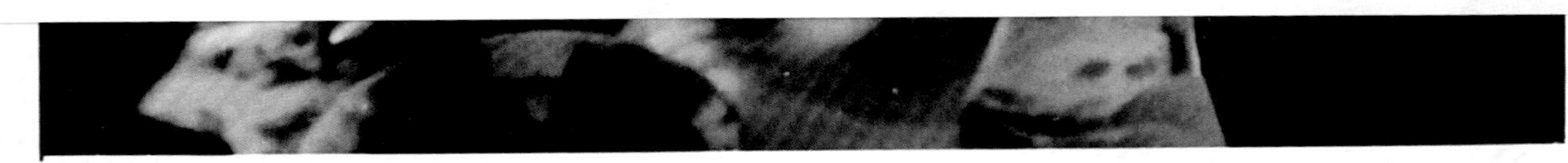

John (right) with Raúl Midence (left), and Luis Coronado Lira (center). Raúl was a member of Castillo Armas's Liberation Army during the coup.

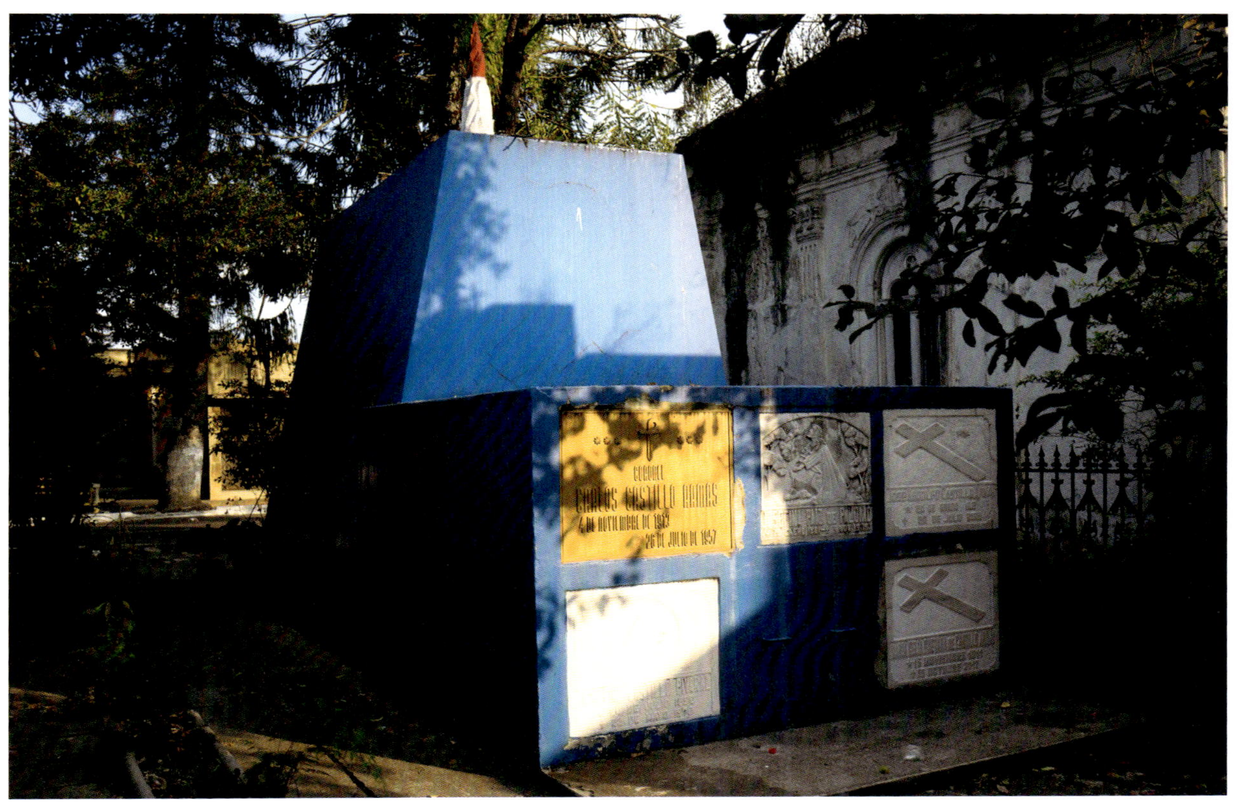

President Carlos Castillo Armas was assassinated by one of his bodyguards in 1957, but his death did not deter the US from influencing future administrations. The events of 1954 were only a foreshadowing of what was to come.

1. China trying to slow down case
   and not permit transfer to
   Tegucigalpa.
2. Reason. — He can try Cuba Judge
   here. Difficult there.
3. Rosales out as Chief of Police.
   Carlos H. Rodriguez replacing him.

Dearest Jo:
        Prensa Libre came out with a
real nice piece about one today!
        If any question is asked you do
not reply. Say only that it is false
and that the courts will decide. Nothing
more. The lawyer says I get out today.
I hope so.
                                Love
                                    John

... care proper protection to
leave country. Otherwise well.
Have had it.
7. Political angles start showing
8. Colon ARGUE-1(A) PR type

I found most of my archival material tucked in a Marshall's shoebox in an old dresser in the basement of my parents' house. The basement had flooded twice but somehow the shoebox had survived. As I sifted through my grandfather's writings, it became clear that he was a consummate professional. He wrote about the weather and asked after the kids, never giving anything away. The only time he broke was in the letter to my grandmother (left), which he had smuggled out of jail in 1962. He was being held on charges of theft, which he believed was a setup. His allies had informed him that there were plans to assassinate him. Who wanted to kill him? I don't know. By then he had Guatemalan enemies. The CIA was tracking him, and several people my grandparents knew had been disappeared. It was the beginning of the Guatemalan Civil War.

While my grandfather was in jail, death threats were made against my mom and her brothers. My grandparents had been threatened before, but never the children. One afternoon, my grandma, dressed in disguise, put the children on a plane to Florida, leaving their home in Guatemala forever. They would miss the death squads that executed and disappeared an estimated 200,000 people, mostly Indigenous, and the rise of rebel groups fighting to restore democracy. Six years later, my grandfather would die in a car accident, one whose circumstances were just as murky as everything else in his life. The official ruling was that he fell asleep at the wheel, but he was standing on the brakes. Growing up, my grandma often spoke about him in such a way that he couldn't possibly be real, either choosing to obscure their difficulties or allowing her memories to soften over time. He was brilliant. Magnanimous. Charming beyond comprehension. My mom, on the other hand, struggled to speak about him at all. As a result, we did little to confront our history with Guatemala. In searching to understand who he was, I had to first grapple with his role in a collective trauma, one still so fresh and simmering that it's palpable when you step off the plane.

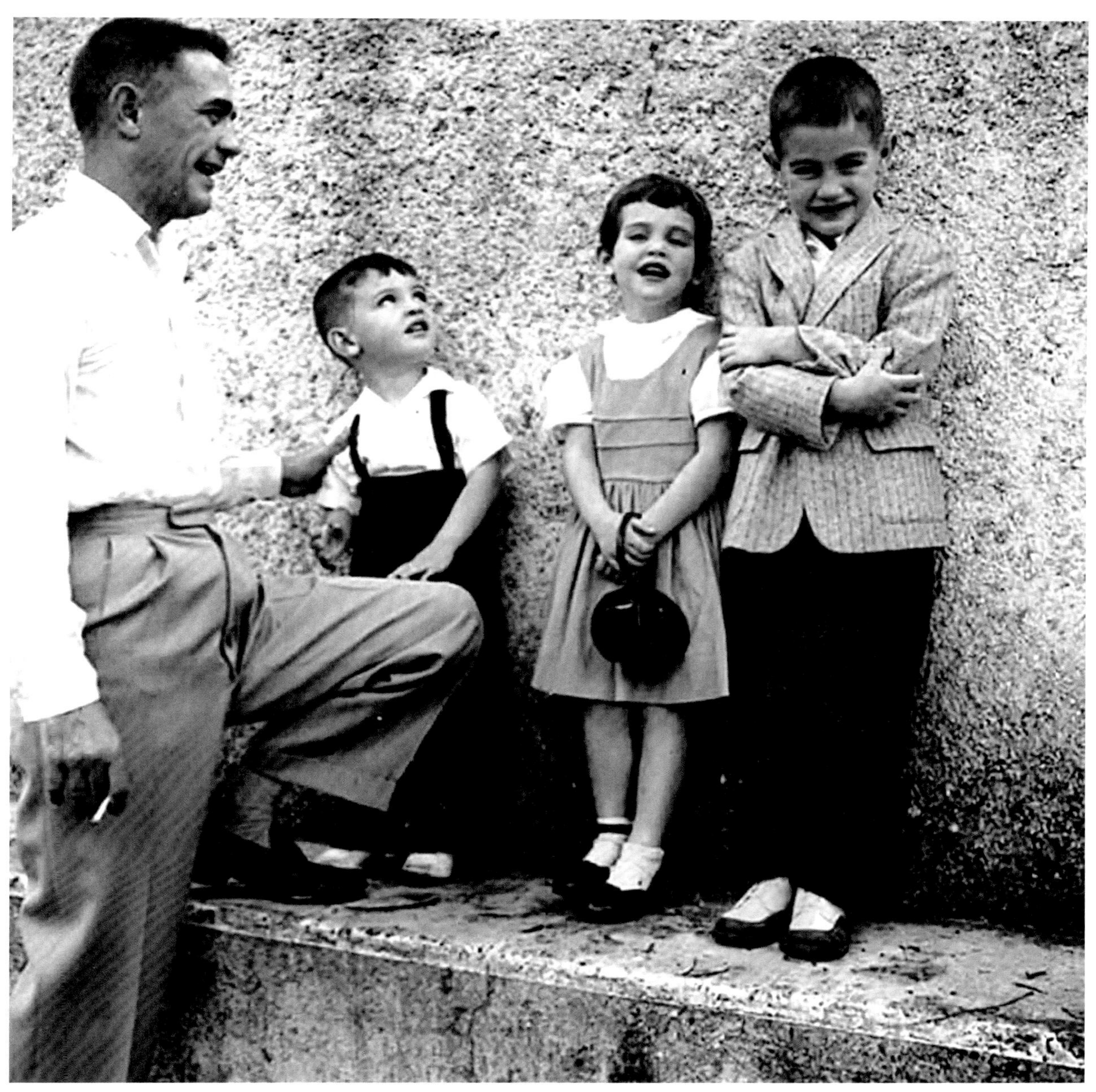

My grandfather, mom and her brothers in Guatemala.

The coup was not the last US intervention in Guatemala, but rather the beginning. The tactics only became more overt. In a declared effort to wage war against Communism, the US funded and trained Guatemala's military, including the now infamous death squads. President Ronald Reagan would rationalize his direct contribution to genocide as collateral damage in counterinsurgency suppression. He would even laud its enforcers. The slaughter of an estimated 200,000 people was sanctioned by Guatemalan President Efraín Ríos Montt, whom President Reagan described in 1982 as "a man of great integrity" and "totally dedicated to democracy." After its successful experiment in Guatemala, the CIA began using its new strategies across Latin America.

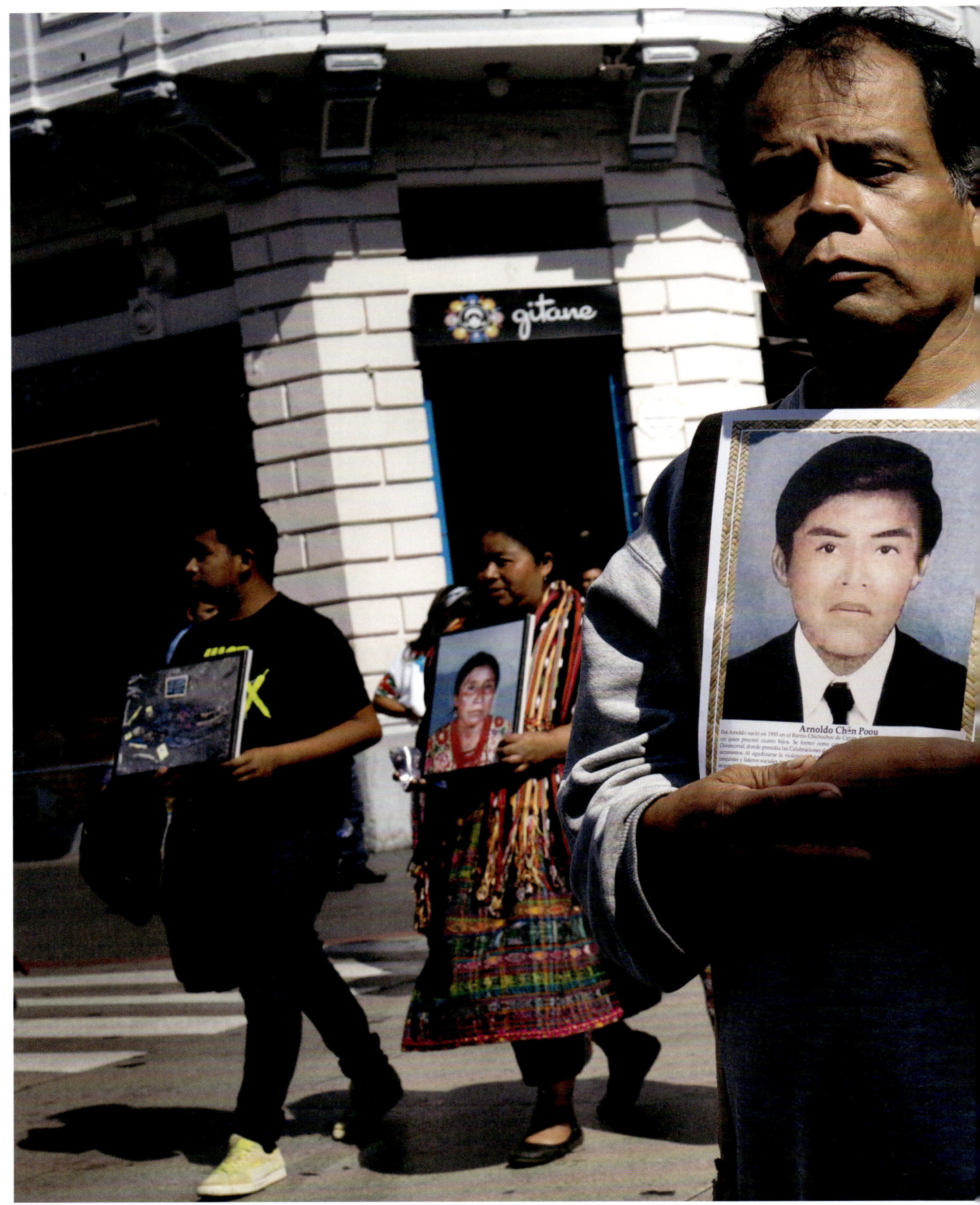
gitane
Arnoldo Chèn Poou
Don Arnoldo nació en 1955 en el Barrio Chichochoc de
con quien procreó cuatro hijos. Se formó como
Chocneoxtal, donde presidía las Celebraciones
sacramentos. Al agudizarse la violencia
catequistas y líderes sociales

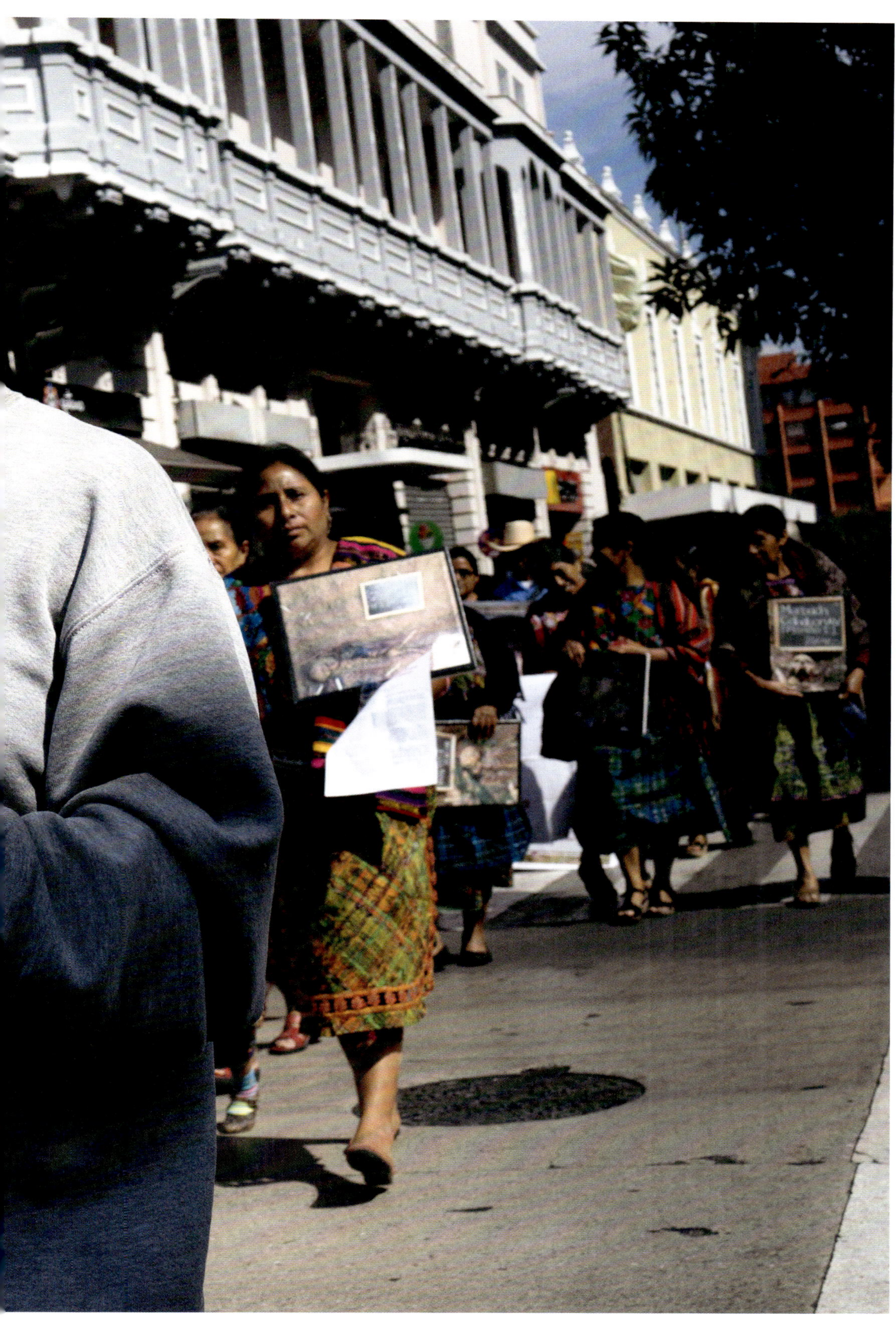

A march for the
disappeared
in Guatemala
City, 2020.
An estimated
45,000
people were
disappeared
by government
forces during
the thirty-
six-year-long
Civil War.

"I'm a product of my father; I'm a product of my grandfather. I participated in nineteen battles. I was in the war; I felt the war. I saw people dying next to me. What I felt, which is something that has accompanied me all my life, was a commitment to Guatemala. It wasn't a romantic feeling; it was a conviction that I was coming to Guatemala to help liberate Guatemala."

—Sandino Asturias Valenzuela

Right: Sandino Asturias Valenzuela was born in exile. His grandfather, Miguel Ángel Asturias Rosales, was a Nobel Prize-winning author and his father, Rodrigo Asturias Amado, was president of the Unidad Revolucionaria Nacional Guatemalteca (URNG) rebel group. Sandino moved to Guatemala to join the URNG and the fight that he believed was his birthright.

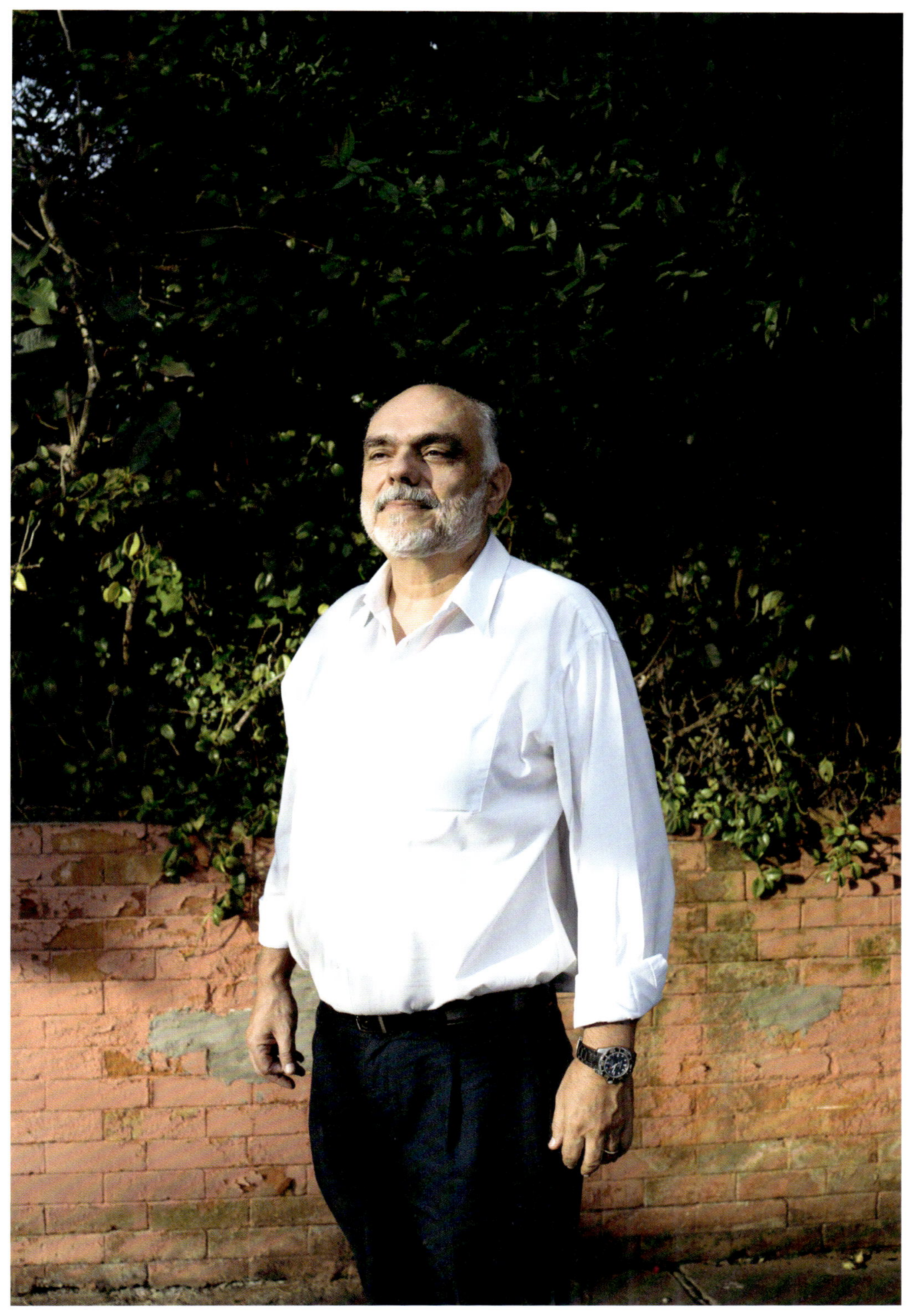

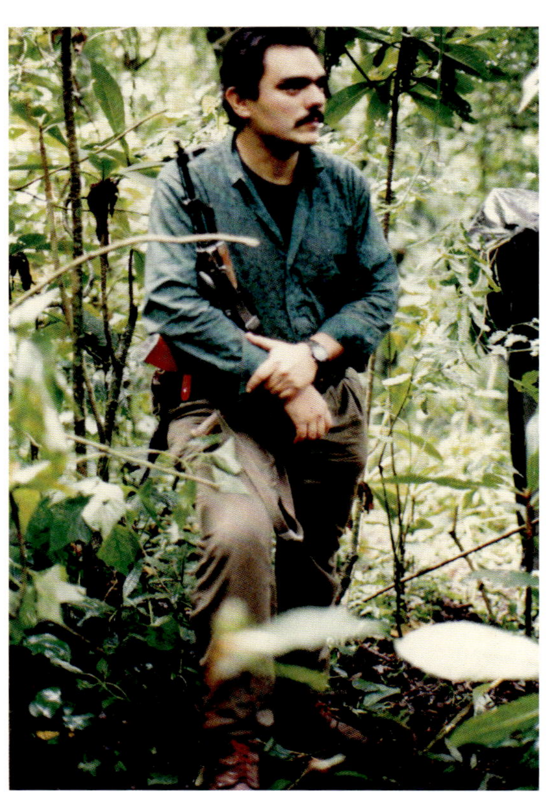

Sandino during the war. This photo was taken moments before an army ambush.

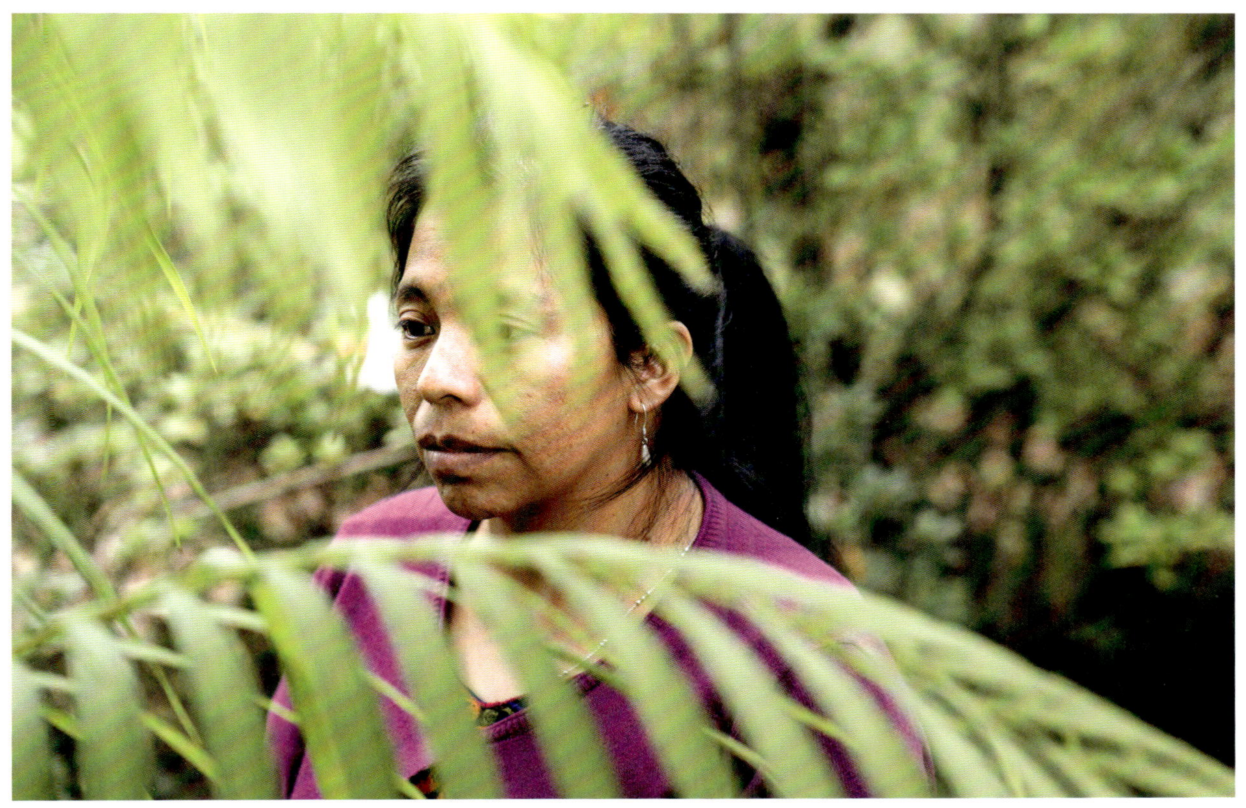

Manuela León was born in 1983 in the middle of the Guatemalan Civil War. Manuela's grandfather was killed by the army, along with several others in her community. Many of the survivors now suffer from alcoholism and PTSD, including her grandmother and father.

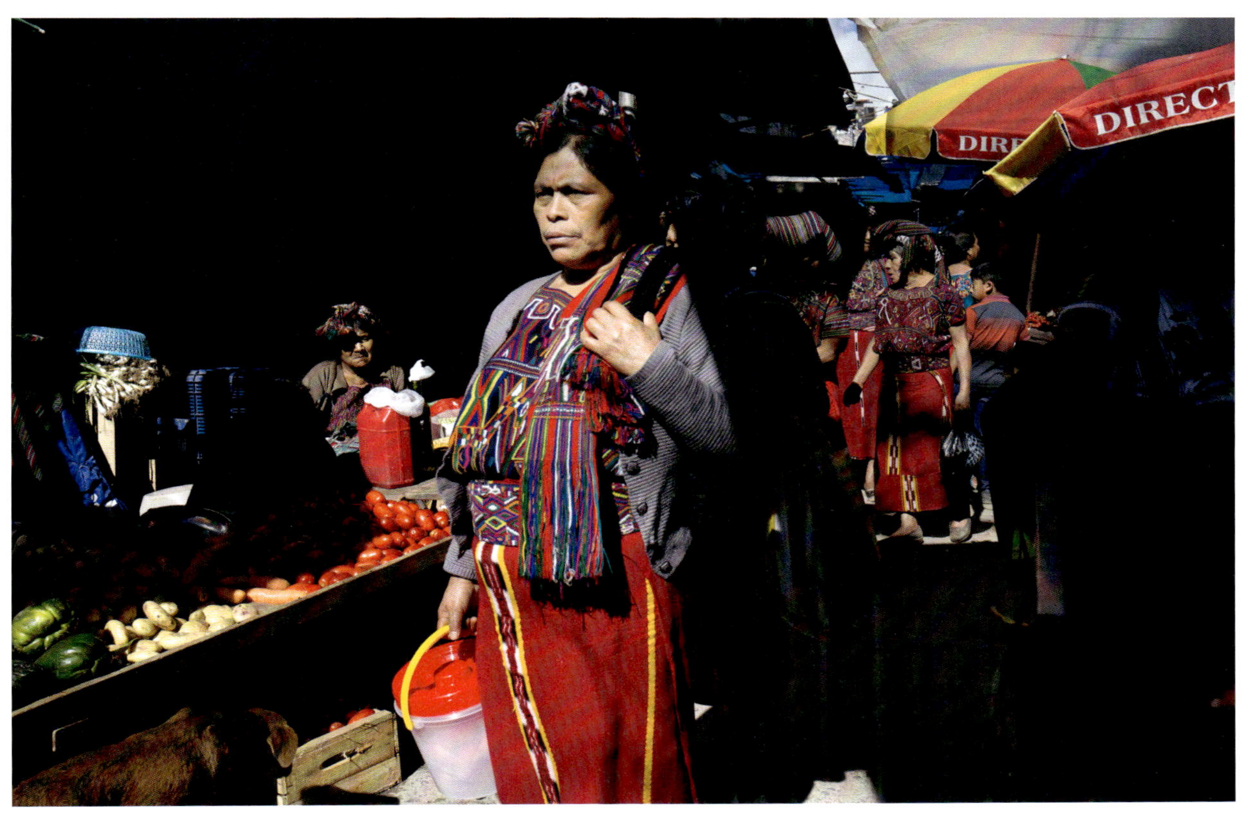

The market in Nebaj, one of the towns most heavily targeted by the death squads during their acts of genocide.

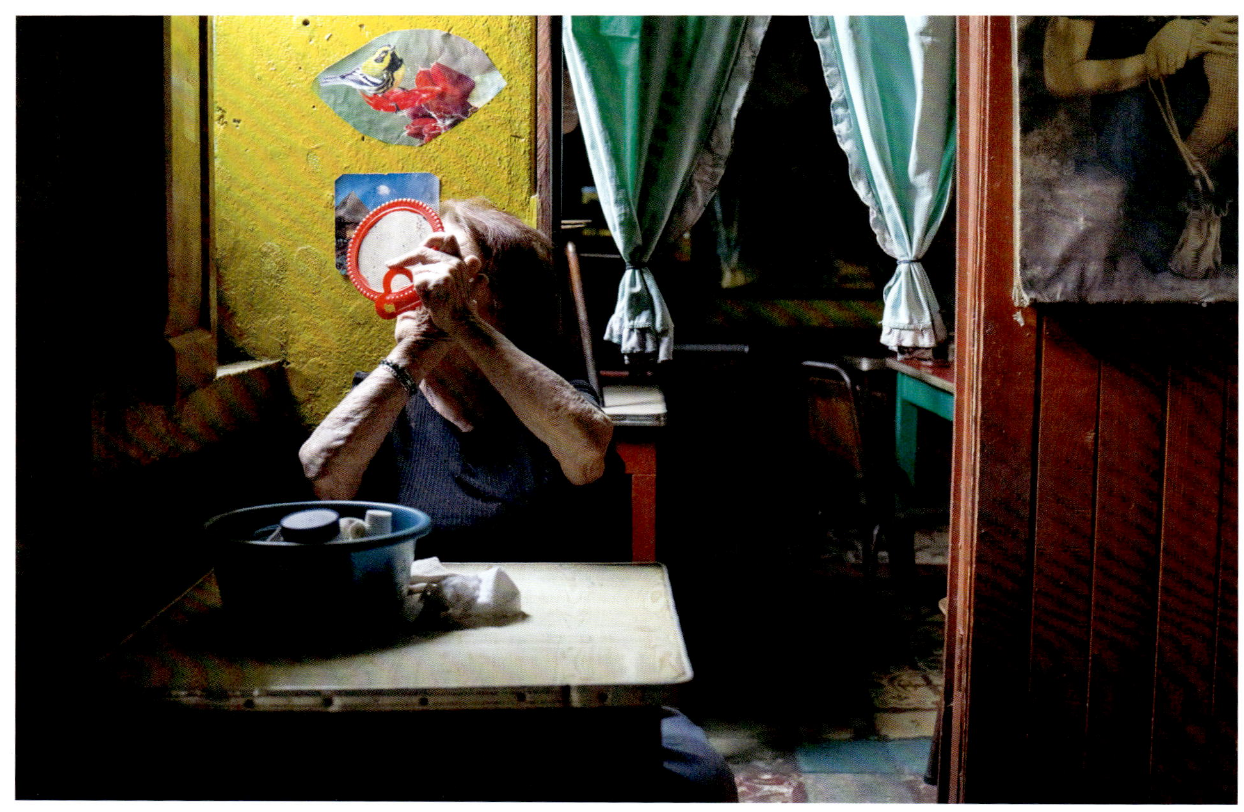

Doña Elsita, preparing to open her bar, El Olvido (The Oblivion). El Olvido was a clandestine meeting spot for guerrillas during the Civil War. Guatemala City, October 2018.

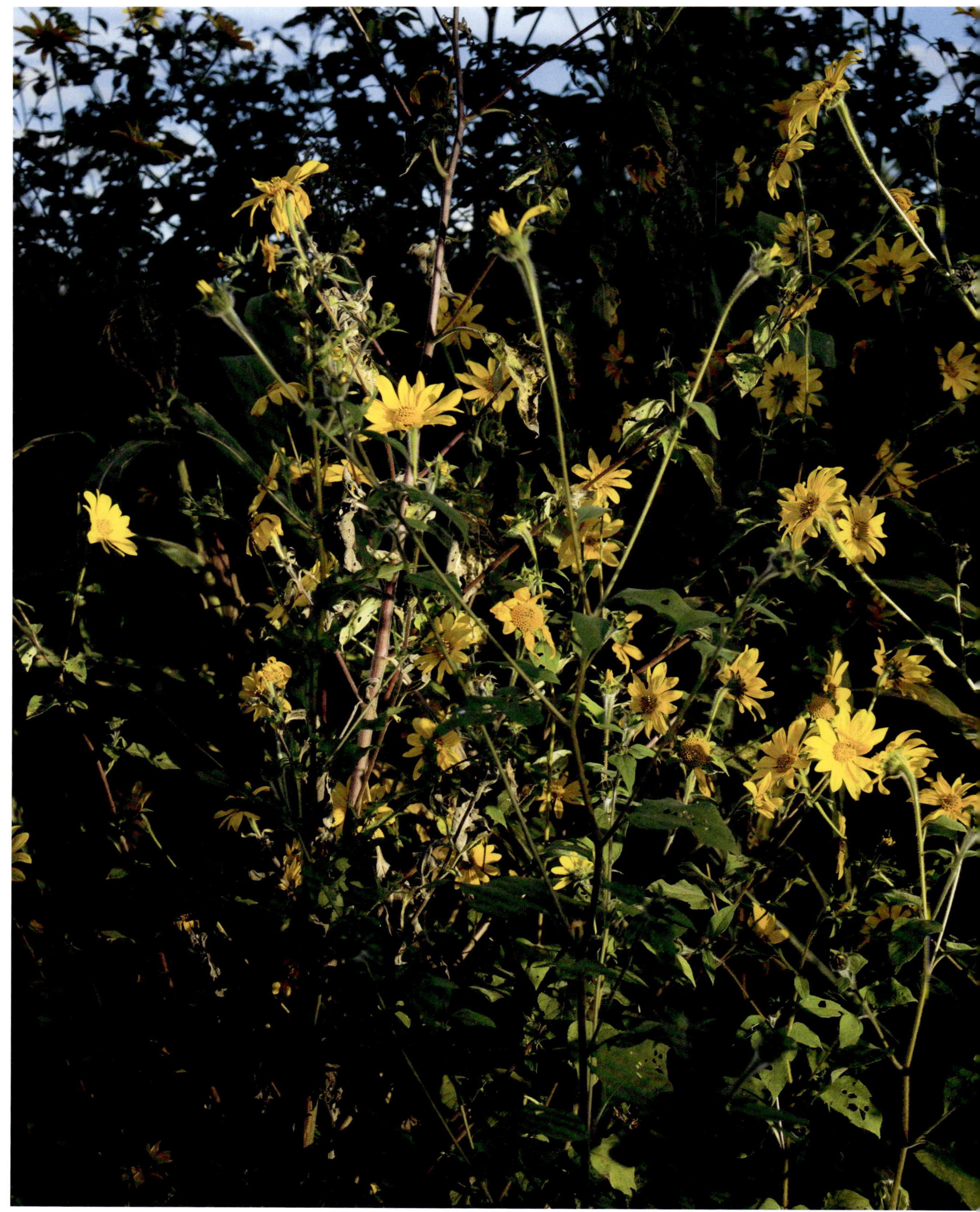

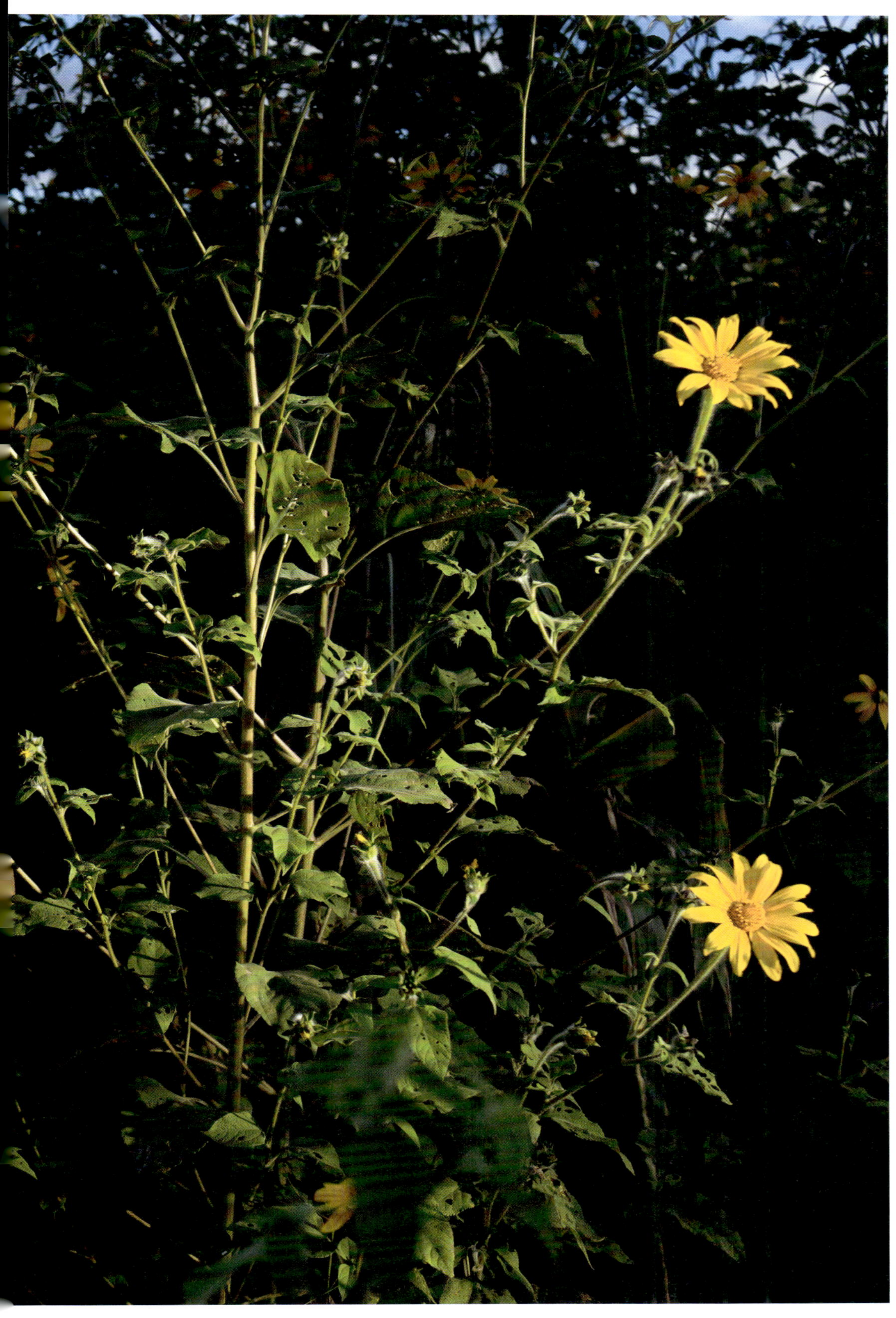

The *flor de muerto* (flower of death) blooms alongside the road near Nebaj, Quiché.

*"The Communist enemy,
real or imagined, became
the target of Castillo
Armas's government. In
'54, state violence was
institutionalized. Although
within the guerrillas there
were crimes, and fighters
who murdered innocent
people, that was not a
guerrilla strategy. It was
not a policy. That's the
difference."*

—Rolando Alecio

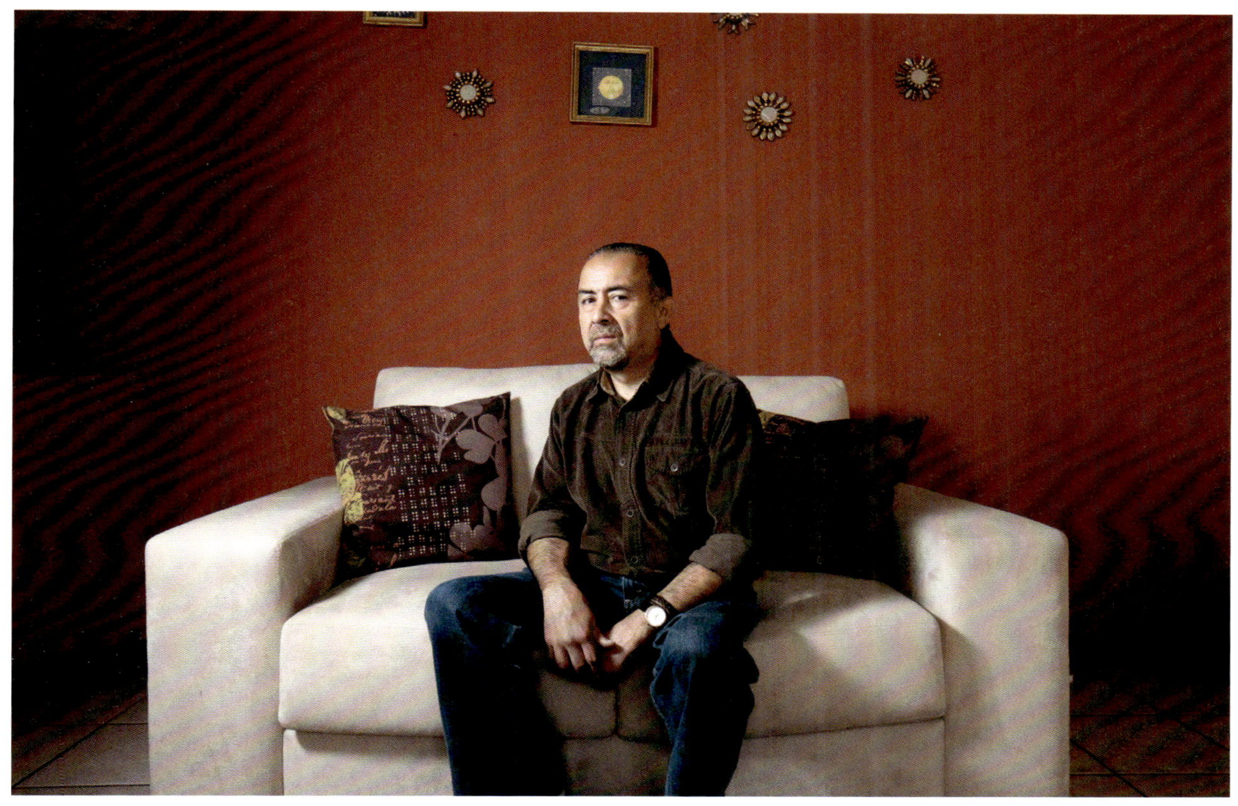

Rolando Alecio is a scholar, activist, and former member of the Fuerzas Armadas Rebeldes guerrilla group. After the Civil War, he worked with organizations providing psychosocial aid for survivors of torture and violence.

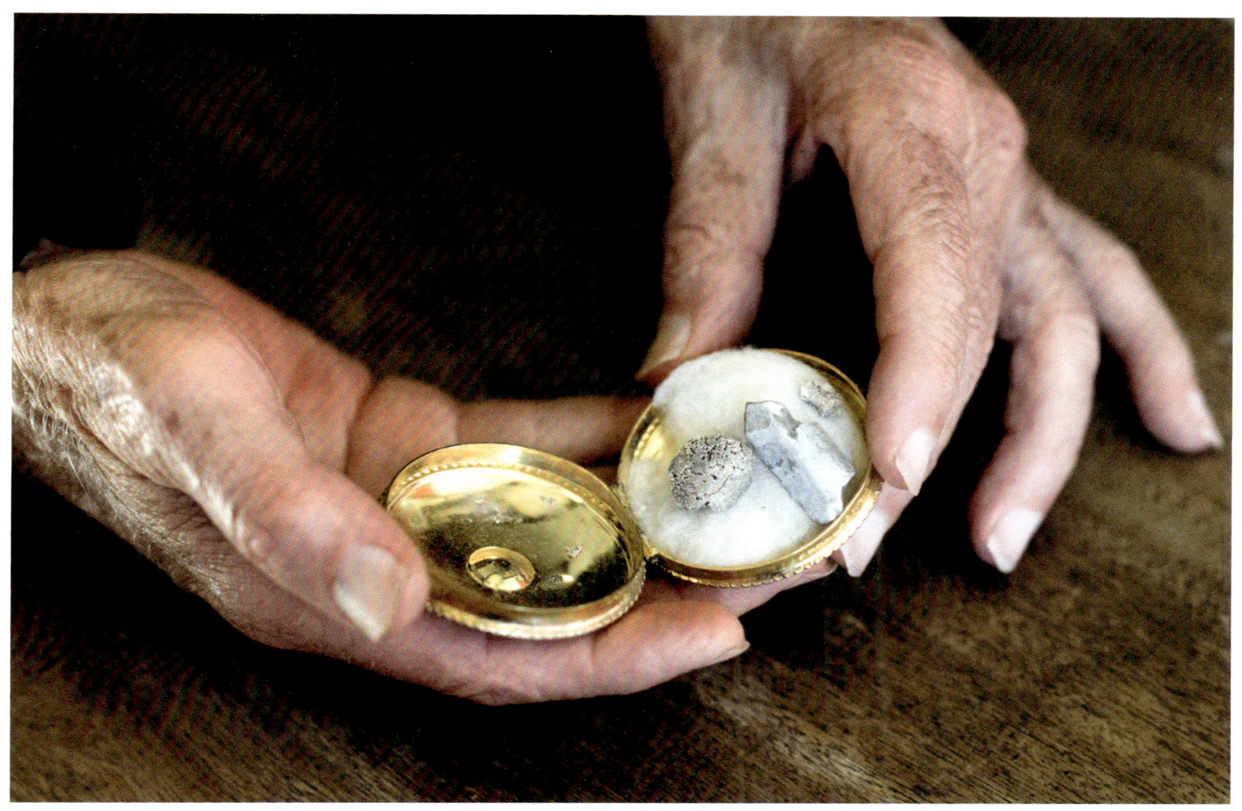

Father Ricardo Falla carries with him a container of human bones from the 1982 massacres in Cuarto Pueblo, Ixcán, a village caught between the guerrillas and the military. All 362 people living in Cuarto Pueblo were killed by the army, and the town was destroyed. Falla keeps the bones with him as a constant reminder of the violence and brutality suffered by the Indigenous peoples.

Right: Julio Solórzano Foppa grew up in exile in Mexico. His mother, María Alaíde Foppa, a well-known poet and writer, and his stepfather, a cabinet adviser to Árbenz, fled Guatemala after the coup. On a return trip to Guatemala in 1980, his mother was disappeared by the military. Then both his brothers, who had joined the guerrillas, were killed.

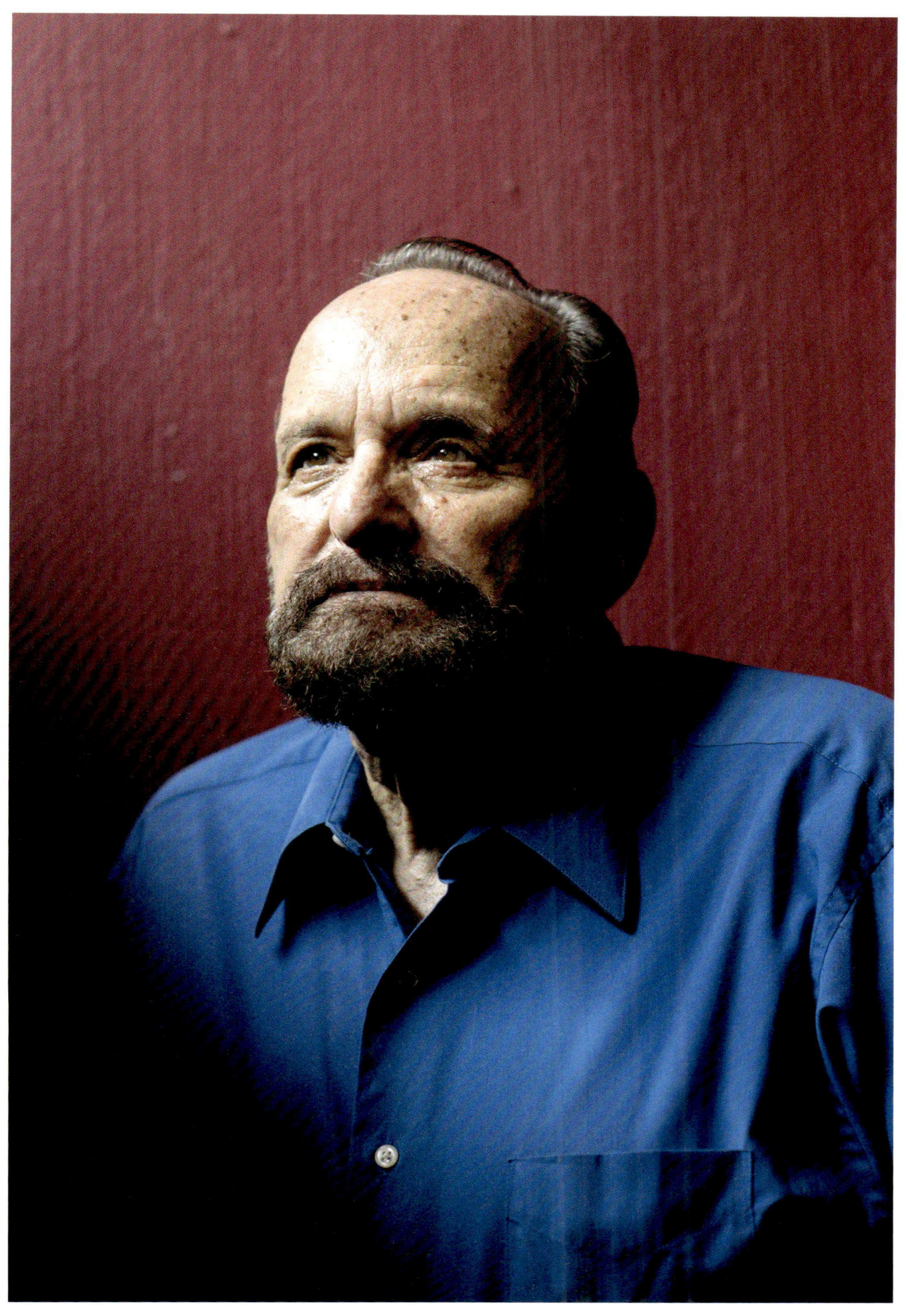

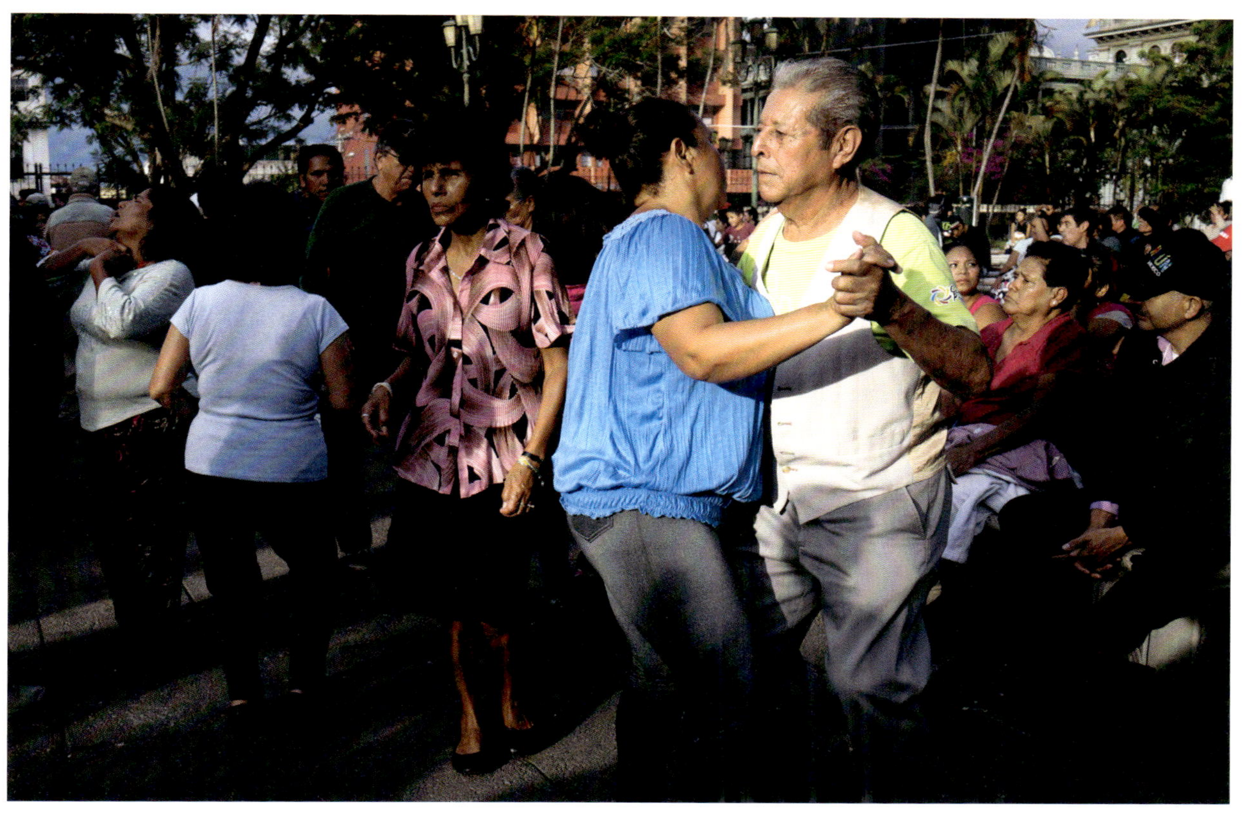

Outside the Palacio Nacional de la Cultura in 2019, fifty-five years after President Árbenz was forced to resign.

Very little of what I thought would connect me to my grandfather actually did. Not the house where the family lived nor the offices where he once worked; not even the children of people who had known him. Instead, I found him in the shadows of my work—in the tangled web that marks Guatemalan politics, the barbed layers of conversations, and my anger as I dug further into our fraught history. I often wondered if he ever came to realize that he had profoundly miscalculated something. Perhaps when he was in jail or as friends were killed or when he struggled to create the dream he'd envisioned. Maybe that's just what I would like to believe. He didn't live long enough to see the long-term effects of the coup, the resulting Civil War that unfolded in its wake. He never saw President Reagan's brutal policy come to life. I'm not sure what he would have thought. My mom thinks that ultimately he would have been on the side of social justice because he was a good man. He had worked for the CIA during the height of the Cold War and that had greatly influenced his perspective. He was doing what he thought was right in the context of his singular role. But how do you reconcile that with the consequences? Do his intentions really matter in the end?

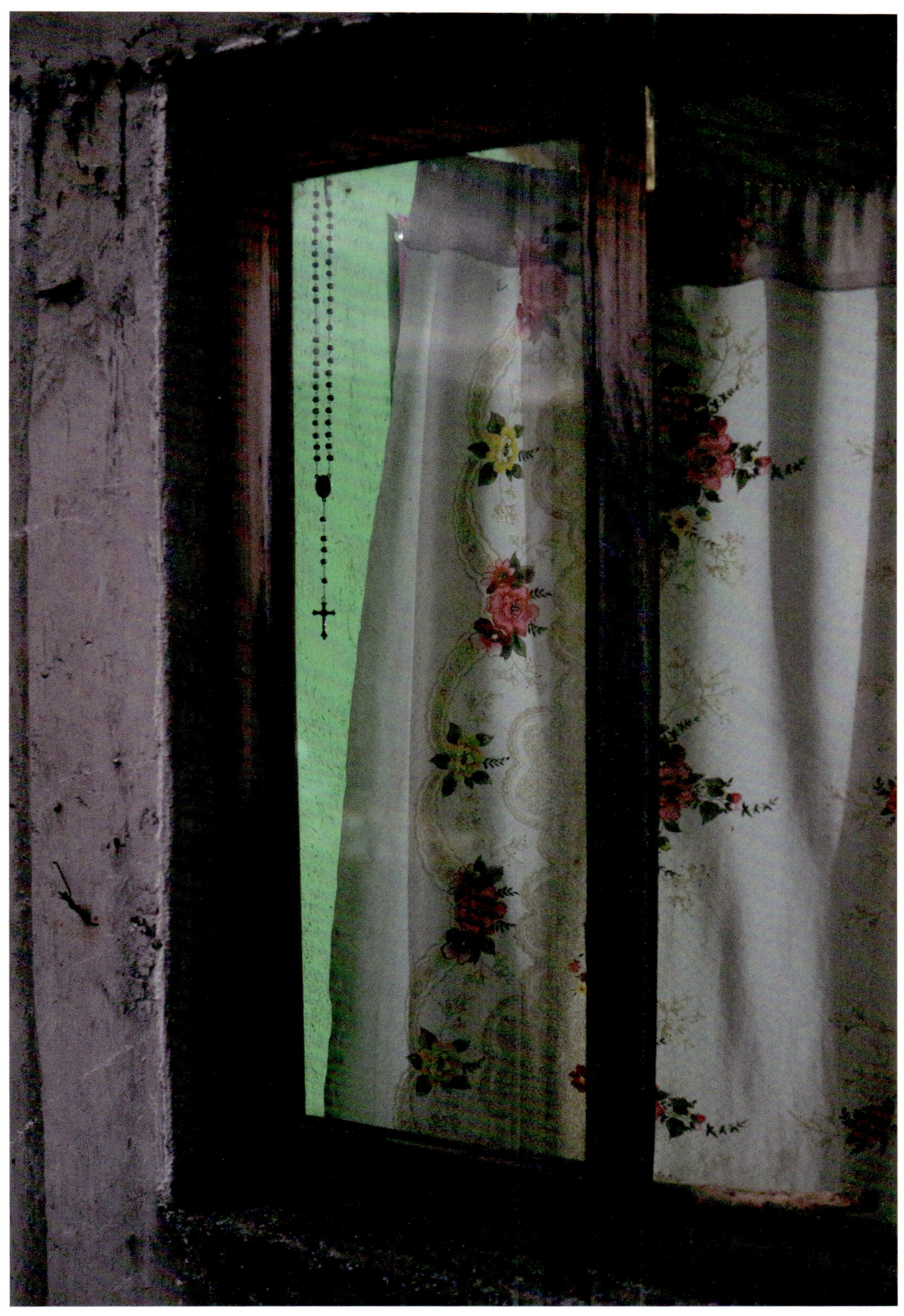

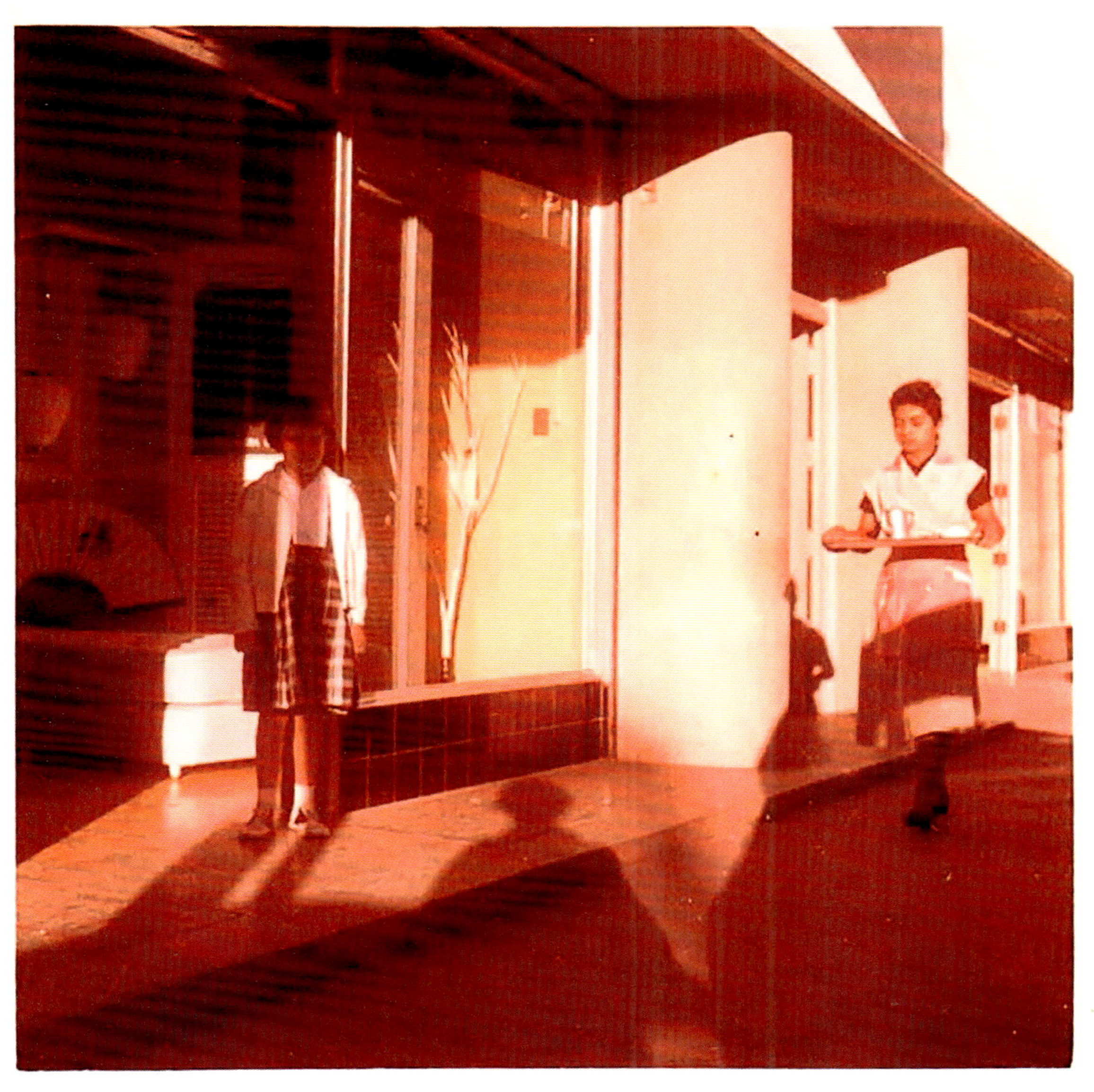

My mom (left) in Guatemala City.

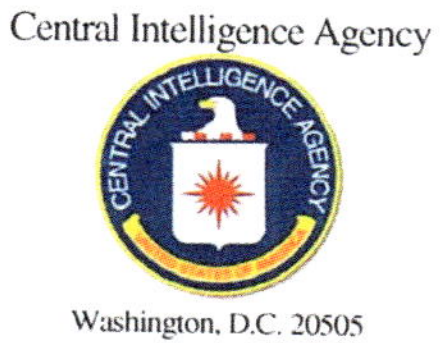

Central Intelligence Agency

Washington, D.C. 20505

28 January 2019

Reference: F-2017-01599

Dear Ms. Dougherty:

This is a final response to your 24 April 2017 Freedom of Information Act (FOIA) request for the personnel records of your parents, **John Solomon Dougherty and Josephine Mary McGlynn**. We processed your request in accordance with the FOIA, 5 U.S.C. § 552, as amended, and the CIA Information Act, 50 U.S.C. § 3141, as amended.

After conducting a search reasonably calculated to uncover all relevant documents, we did not locate any responsive records that would reveal an openly acknowledged CIA affiliation with the subject.

To the extent that your request also seeks records that would reveal a classified association between the CIA and the subject, if any exist, we can neither confirm nor deny having such records, pursuant to Section 3.6(a) of Executive Order 13526, as amended. If a classified association between the subject and this organization were to exist, records revealing such a relationship would be properly classified and require continued safeguards against unauthorized disclosure. You may consider this finding a denial of this portion of your request pursuant to FOIA exemptions (b)(1) and (b)(3). Exemption (b)(3) pertains to information exempt from disclosure by statute. In this case, the relevant statutes are Section 6 of the Central Intelligence Agency Act of 1949, 50 U.S.C. § 3507, as amended, and Section 102A(i)(1) of the National Security Act of 1947, 50 U.S.C. 3024(i)(1), as amended. I have enclosed an explanation of exemptions for your reference and retention. As the CIA Information and Privacy Coordinator, I am the CIA official responsible for this determination. You have the right to appeal this response to the Agency Release Panel, in my care, within 90 days from the date of this letter. Please include the basis of your appeal.

If you have any questions regarding our response, you may contact us at:

Central Intelligence Agency
Washington, DC 20505
Information and Privacy Coordinator
703-613-3007 (Fax)

ON HISTORICAL MEMORY

An excerpt from a conversation with Julio Solórzano Foppa (pictured on page 109).

WHAT IS THE RELATIONSHIP BETWEEN HISTORICAL MEMORY AND THE TRUTH?

They're both very subjective concepts. If a situation can be seen and understood from different perspectives, then your truth can be very different. Historical memory is the same. There's a certain amount of facts, but they can be interpreted in many ways. When you try to be objective, meaning going to the facts without judging or qualifying, it's almost impossible. So it's good to have different versions of the same events so that whoever is looking can make up their own mind.

YOU MENTIONED THAT EVEN AMONGST YOUR SIBLINGS, YOU PERCEIVE CERTAIN EVENTS DIFFERENTLY. YOU HAVE A DIFFERENT LENS ON HISTORY. HOW DO YOU RECONCILE THAT?

I'm not looking to reconcile anything. I respect how they think. I try to understand. We just have a different view of the same events. I think to your first question, what is true to me, it is not necessarily true to them and vice versa.

WHAT DOES IT MEAN TO HEAL, AS A COUNTRY AND AS AN INDIVIDUAL?

I think they're two different things. It's a very personal and individual process. But as a country, the only road to healing is justice, both in terms of justice against those who committed crimes, but also economical justice. There are people in this country that deserve a lot more than what they've gotten historically. There should be a system that provides more opportunities for people to develop their lives without having to look for work in the United States or become part of organized crime.

ACKNOWLEDGMENTS

This work is a culmination of many people's efforts. Specifically, it was made in collaboration with the people who agreed to fix on my behalf, whose knowledge, talent, and leadership influenced the work: Xiomara Rivas, Alejandro Ariazza Ibarra, Morena Pérez Joachin, and Trudy Mercadal.

I would also like to thank Anna Watts, Dane Jones, Sharon Pulwer, Kathleen Head, Jess Honeywell, Bob Nickelsberg, Rob Grossinger, John B. Dougherty, and Kevin Dougherty for their expertise, review, and logistical support.

But most of all, I'd like to thank my mom, Maren Dougherty, who gave me unwavering support and creative freedom to examine a painful family story. The fact that this book exists is a testament to her love.